Easy Asian

A classic kitchen collection for the busy cook

MURDOCH BOOKS

Contents

6 Thai chicken rolls

7 Crispy lamb with lettuce

9 Vegetable tempura patties

Small
bites

Thai chicken rolls

»PREPARATION 25 MINUTES »COOKING TIME 10 MINUTES »MAKES 30

1 Put the chicken, lemon grass, chilli, shallots, mint, coriander, fish sauce and lime juice in a food processor and process to combine.

2 Cut thirty rectangles, 10 x 16 cm (4 x 6¼ inches), from the tofu skins and lightly brush them with water to soften. Roll about 1 tablespoon of the chicken mixture into a log and place on each tofu rectangle. Roll up from the short end, folding in the ends as you roll.

3 Fill a wok or deep heavy-based saucepan one-third full of oil and heat to 180°C (350°F/Gas 4), or until a cube of bread dropped into the oil browns in 15 seconds. Deep-fry the rolls in batches for 1 minute, or until golden brown. If the tofu skin is browning before the chicken is cooked, turn the heat down. Drain well on crumpled paper towels. Serve garnished with shredded makrut leaves.

600 g (1 lb 5 oz) minced (ground) chicken
4 lemon grass stems, white part only, finely chopped
4 red chillies, seeded and finely chopped
6 red Asian shallots, finely chopped
2 tablespoons chopped Vietnamese mint
3 tablespoons finely chopped coriander (cilantro) leaves
2 tablespoons fish sauce
2 tablespoons lime juice
100 g (3½ oz) packet tofu skins
oil, for deep-frying
4 makrut (kaffir lime) leaves, finely shredded, to garnish

Crispy lamb with lettuce

»PREPARATION 15 MINUTES + 3 HOURS REFRIGERATION »COOKING TIME 20 MINUTES »SERVES 4

1 Wrap the lamb in plastic wrap. Put it in the freezer for 30 minutes, or until semi-frozen. Cut the lamb lengthways into three thin slices, then thinly slice across the grain so that you have julienne strips. Place in a bowl with the soy sauce, rice wine, fish sauce, sesame oil, garlic and ginger. Mix well to coat, then cover and refrigerate for 2 hours.

2 Sift the cornflour over the lamb and mix well. Spread the lamb out on a tray and refrigerate, uncovered, for 1 hour.

3 Preheat the oven to 150°C (300°F/Gas 2). Heat the oil in a wok or deep heavy-based saucepan to 180°C (350°F/Gas 4), or until a cube of bread dropped into the oil browns in 15 seconds. Deep-fry the lamb in batches for 5–6 minutes, or until crisp and browned. Lift the lamb out with a slotted spoon and drain on crumpled paper towel. Keep warm in the oven while you cook the remainder.

4 To serve, cup a lettuce leaf in one hand. With the other hand, drizzle the inside with a little plum sauce, fill with the lamb and sprinkle with spring onion. Alternatively, arrange the lettuce, lamb, spring onion and plum sauce in separate dishes for your guests to assemble themselves.

400 g (14 oz) lamb backstraps or loin fillets
2 tablespoons light soy sauce
1 tablespoon Chinese rice wine
2 teaspoons fish sauce
½ teaspoon sesame oil
2 garlic cloves, crushed
1 teaspoon finely grated fresh ginger
40 g (1½ oz/⅓ cup) cornflour (cornstarch)
oil, for deep-frying
12 baby cos lettuce leaves
plum sauce, to serve
4 spring onions (scallions), thinly sliced, to serve

Prawn gow gees

»PREPARATION 40 MINUTES + 1 HOUR REFRIGERATION »COOKING TIME 15 MINUTES »MAKES 24

1 Peel the prawns and gently pull out the dark vein from each prawn back, starting from the head end. Finely chop the prawn meat.

2 Mix the chopped prawns, pork, spring onion, bamboo shoots, egg white, ginger, sesame oil, white pepper and 1 teaspoon salt in a bowl until well combined. Cover with plastic wrap and refrigerate for at least 1 hour.

3 Put one gow gee wrapper on a work surface and place 2 teaspoons of the filling in the centre. Position the filling in an oblong across the wrapper, rather than a round lump. Dip your finger in water and lightly moisten the edge of the wrapper. Pick up the wrapper and fold the edges together to form a semi-circle.

Using your thumb and index finger, create a row of pleats along the outside edge, pressing firmly. Twist the corners down to seal and form a crescent shape. Make sure the gow gee is completely sealed so that the filling doesn't leak during steaming. Repeat with the remaining wrappers and filling to make 24 gow gees.

4 Line a double bamboo steamer with baking paper. Arrange the gow gees in the steamer in a single layer, leaving a gap between each one. Cover and steam over simmering water for 8 minutes, or until the gow gees are cooked through.

5 Meanwhile, to make the dipping sauce, combine the soy sauce, red vinegar and sesame oil. Serve with the hot gow gees.

300 g (10½ oz) raw prawns (shrimp)
100 g (3½ oz) minced (ground) pork
4 spring onions (scallions), white part only, finely chopped
25 g (1 oz) tinned bamboo shoots, finely chopped
1 egg white
1 teaspoon finely chopped fresh ginger
1 teaspoon sesame oil
¼ teaspoon ground white pepper
24 round gow gee wrappers

Dipping sauce
60 ml (2 fl oz/¼ cup) soy sauce
1 tablespoon Chinese red vinegar
¼ teaspoon sesame oil

Vegetable tempura patties

» PREPARATION 25 MINUTES » COOKING TIME 15 MINUTES » SERVES 4

1 To make the wasabi mayonnaise, combine the ingredients in a small bowl. Keep refrigerated until ready to serve.

2 Put the zucchini, potato, carrot, onion, sweet potato, spring onion and nori in a bowl. Toss together.

3 Sift the tempura flour into a large bowl and make a well in the centre. Add the soda water and loosely mix together with chopsticks or a fork until just combined — the batter should still be lumpy. Add all of the vegetables and quickly fold through to coat.

4 Fill a wok or large heavy-based saucepan one-third full of oil and heat to 180°C (350°F/Gas 4), or until a cube of bread dropped into the oil browns in 15 seconds. Gently drop 60 g (2¼ oz/¼ cup) of the vegetable mixture into oil, making sure that the patty is not too compact, and cook for 1–2 minutes, or until golden and crisp. Drain patties on crumpled paper towel. Repeat with remaining mixture.

5 Season with sea salt and then serve immediately with the wasabi mayonnaise and pickled ginger.

Wasabi mayonnaise
125 g (4½ oz/½ cup) whole-egg mayonnaise
2 teaspoons wasabi paste
1 teaspoon Japanese soy sauce
1 teaspoon sake

1 small zucchini (courgette), grated
1 small potato, cut into matchsticks
½ carrot, cut into matchsticks
½ onion, thinly sliced
100 g (3½ oz) orange sweet potato, grated
4 spring onions (scallions), cut into 2 cm (¾ inch) lengths
4 nori sheets, shredded
250 g (9 oz/2 cups) tempura flour, sifted
500 ml (17 fl oz/2 cups) chilled soda water
oil, for deep-frying
2 tablespoons shredded pickled ginger, to serve

Spring rolls

»PREPARATION 45 MINUTES »COOKING TIME 20 MINUTES »MAKES 30

1 Put the dried mushrooms in a heatproof bowl, cover with boiling water and soak for 20 minutes. Squeeze the mushrooms dry, then discard the stems and thinly slice the caps.

2 Mix the pork, soy sauce, sherry, five-spice and 1 tablespoon of the cornflour in a non-metallic bowl. Leave for 15 minutes.

3 Heat 2 tablespoons of the peanut oil in a wok over high heat until nearly smoking. Stir-fry the celery, spring onion, bamboo shoots and Chinese cabbage for 3–4 minutes, until just soft. Season with salt, then transfer to a bowl and set aside.

4 Heat the remaining peanut oil in the wok and stir-fry the garlic and ginger for 30 seconds. Add the pork mixture and stir-fry for 2–3 minutes, or until nearly cooked. Combine 1½ teaspoons of the cornflour with 60 ml (2 fl oz/¼ cup) water. Return the vegetables to the wok, then stir in the mushrooms. Add the sugar, sesame oil and cornflour mixture and cook, stirring, for 2 minutes. Remove from the heat and cool.

5 To make the dipping sauce, combine the soy sauce, hoisin sauce, plum sauce, sweet chilli sauce and 80 ml (2½ fl oz/⅓ cup) water in a bowl and stir to combine.

6 Combine the remaining cornflour with 2–3 teaspoons of cold water to make a paste. Place one spring roll wrapper on a work surface, with one corner pointing towards you. Put 2 teaspoons of the filling in the centre of the wrapper, then brush the edges with a little of the paste. Roll up, tucking in the sides as you do so. Repeat with the remaining filling and wrappers.

7 Fill a wok or deep heavy-based saucepan one-third full of oil and heat to 180°C (350°F/Gas 4), or until a cube of bread dropped into the oil browns in 15 seconds. Deep-fry spring rolls in batches until golden. Drain on crumpled paper towel and serve hot with dipping sauce.

2 dried shiitake mushrooms

250 g (9 oz) minced (ground) pork

1½ tablespoons dark soy sauce

2 teaspoons dry sherry

½ teaspoon Chinese five-spice

2 tablespoons cornflour (cornstarch),
plus 1½ teaspoons, extra

80 ml (2½ fl oz/⅓ cup) peanut oil

½ celery stalk, finely chopped

2 spring onions (scallions), thinly sliced

30 g (1 oz) tinned bamboo shoots,
finely sliced

40 g (1½ oz/¾ cup) shredded Chinese
cabbage (wong bok)

2 garlic cloves, crushed

2 teaspoons finely chopped fresh
ginger

¼ teaspoon sugar

¼ teaspoon sesame oil

250 g (9 oz) packet 12 cm (4½ inch)
square spring roll wrappers

oil, for deep-frying

Dipping sauce

2 tablespoons soy sauce

1 tablespoon hoisin sauce

1 tablespoon plum sauce

1 tablespoon sweet chilli sauce

Teppan yaki

»PREPARATION 45 MINUTES »COOKING TIME 25 MINUTES »SERVES 4

1 Thinly slice 350 g (12 oz) partially frozen scotch fillet. Place the meat in a single layer on a large serving platter, season well and set aside.

2 Cut 4 small slender eggplants (aubergines) into long, thin diagonal slices. Top and tail 10 g (3½ oz) of small green beans, and halve them if long. Trim the hard stems from 100 g (3½ oz) fresh shiitake mushrooms. Quarter or halve 6 baby (pattypan) yellow or green squash. Cut 1 red or green capsicum (pepper) into strips. Slice 6 spring onions (scallions) into 7 cm (2¾ inches) lengths, discarding the tops. Drain 200 g (7 oz) tinned bamboo shoots. Arrange all the vegetables in bundles on a plate.

3 When the diners are seated, heat an electric grill or electric frying pan until very hot and lightly brush it with oil. Quickly fry a quarter of the meat, searing on both sides, and then push it over to the edge of the pan. Add about a quarter of the vegetables and quickly stir-fry, adding a little more oil as needed. Serve a small portion of the meat and vegetables to the diners, who dip the food into a sauce of their choice. Repeat the process with the remaining meat and vegetables, cooking in batches as extra helpings are required. Serve the teppan yaki with steamed rice.

Samosas

»PREPARATION 30 MINUTES »COOKING TIME 25 MINUTES »MAKES 24

1 To make the cucumber raita, put the cucumber and yoghurt in a bowl and mix together well. Dry-fry the cumin and mustard seeds in a small frying pan over medium heat for 1 minute, or until fragrant and lightly browned. Add to the yoghurt mixture. Stir in the ginger, season to taste with salt and freshly ground black pepper, and mix together well. Refrigerate until needed.

2 Heat a wok over medium heat, add the oil and swirl to coat the base and side. Add the onion, ginger and garlic. Cook for 2 minutes, or until softened, then add the spices, boiled potato, peas and 2 teaspoons water. Cook for 1 minute, or until all the moisture evaporates. Remove from the heat and stir in the coriander leaves and lemon juice.

3 Cut 12 rounds from the pastry sheets using a 12.5 cm (5 inch) cutter, then cut each round in half. Shape 1 semi-circle into a cone, wet the edges and seal the side seam, leaving an opening for the filling. Spoon 3 teaspoons of the filling into the cone, then seal. Repeat to make 24 samosas.

4 Fill a wok or deep heavy-based saucepan one-third full of oil and heat to 180°C (350°F/Gas 4), or until a cube of bread dropped into the oil browns in 15 seconds. Cook the samosas in batches for 1–2 minutes, or until golden. Drain on crumpled paper towel and season. Serve with chilled cucumber raita.

Note Raita can be made ahead of time and stored in the refrigerator in an airtight container for up to 3 days.

Cucumber raita
2 Lebanese (short) cucumbers, peeled, seeded and finely chopped
250 g (9 oz/1 cup) plain yoghurt
1 teaspoon ground cumin
1 teaspoon mustard seeds
½ teaspoon grated fresh ginger

1 tablespoon vegetable oil
1 onion, chopped
1 teaspoon grated fresh ginger
1 garlic clove, crushed
2 teaspoons ground coriander
2 teaspoons ground cumin
2 teaspoons garam masala
1½ teaspoons chilli powder
¼ teaspoon ground turmeric
300 g (10½ oz) potatoes, cut into 1 cm (½ inch) cubes and boiled
40 g (1½ oz/⅓ cup) frozen peas
2 tablespoons chopped coriander (cilantro) leaves
1 teaspoon lemon juice
6 sheets ready-rolled puff pastry
oil, for deep-frying

Spiced prawn pakoras

»PREPARATION 20 MINUTES »COOKING TIME 10 MINUTES »MAKES 16

1 Peel the prawns and gently pull out the dark vein from each prawn back, starting from the head end, leaving the tails intact.

2 Sift the besan, baking powder and spices into a large bowl and season with a little salt. Make a well in the centre, then gradually add 250 ml (9 fl oz/1 cup) of water and gently stir until combined. Beat the egg white until firm peaks form and then fold into the batter.

3 Fill a wok one-third full of oil and heat to 180°C (350°F/Gas 4), or until a cube of bread dropped into the oil browns in 15 seconds. Using the tail as a handle, dip the prawns into the batter, then lower gently into the oil. Deep-fry the prawns in batches, until the batter is lightly golden; it won't become really crisp. Drain on crumpled paper towel.

4 To make the dipping sauce, combine the yoghurt, coriander and cumin. Sprinkle with garam masala and serve with the pakoras.

16 raw prawns (shrimp)
85 g (3 oz/¾ cup) besan (chickpea flour)
½ teaspoon baking powder
¼ teaspoon ground turmeric
1 teaspoon ground coriander
½ teaspoon ground cumin
½ teaspoon chilli powder
oil, for deep-frying
1 tablespoon egg white

Dipping sauce
250 g (9 oz/1 cup) plain yoghurt
3 tablespoons chopped coriander (cilantro) leaves
1 teaspoon ground cumin
garam masala, to sprinkle

Salt and pepper squid

»PREPARATION 30 MINUTES »COOKING TIME 10 MINUTES »SERVES 10

1 Open out the squid tubes, wash and pat dry. Lay the squid on a chopping board with the inside facing upwards. Score a diamond pattern on the squid, being careful not to cut all the way through. Cut into 5 x 3 cm (2 x 1¼ inch) pieces. Place in a flat non-metallic dish and pour the lemon juice over. Cover and refrigerate for 15 minutes. Drain and pat dry.

2 Combine the cornflour, white pepper, sugar and 1 tablespoon salt in a bowl. Dip the squid pieces into the egg white and then dust with the flour mixture.

3 Fill a wok or deep heavy-based saucepan one-third full of oil and heat to 180°C (350°F/Gas 4), or until a cube of bread dropped into the oil browns in 15 seconds. Deep-fry the squid in batches for 1–2 minutes, until the squid turns white and curls. Drain on crumpled paper towel and serve immediately with lemon wedges and coriander.

1 kg (2 lb 4 oz) squid tubes, halved lengthways
250 ml (9 fl oz/1 cup) lemon juice
250 g (9 oz/2 cups) cornflour (cornstarch)
1 tablespoon ground white pepper
2 teaspoons caster (superfine) sugar
4 egg whites, lightly beaten
oil, for deep-frying
lemon wedges, to serve
coriander (cilantro) leaves, to garnish

Scallop dumplings

»PREPARATION 30 MINUTES + 4 HOURS REFRIGERATION »COOKING TIME 10 MINUTES »MAKES 24

1 Cut 250 g (9 oz) of snow pea (mangetout) sprouts into 1 cm (½ inch) pieces. Bring a saucepan of salted water to the boil, add the snow pea sprouts and ½ teaspoon bicarbonate of soda (baking soda) and blanch for 10 seconds. Refresh under cold water, then drain until thoroughly dry.

2 Put 250 g (9 oz) white scallop meat in a food processor bowl with 1 teaspoon of finely grated fresh ginger, 1½ tablespoons of oyster sauce, 1 teaspoon of Chinese rice wine, 1 teaspoon of light soy sauce and ½ teaspoon of sesame oil. Add 1½ teaspoons of sugar, 1 teaspoon of cornflour (cornstarch), 1 egg white and ¼ teaspoon of salt and blend until evenly mixed. Transfer to a bowl, cover and refrigerate for 4 hours. Add the snow pea sprouts and mix thoroughly.

3 Place 2 teaspoons of filling in the centre of a gow gee wrapper, then wet the edges and gather together to cover the filling. Squeeze shut, making a round bundle. Break off any surplus dough. Repeat to make 24 dumplings. Line a double bamboo steamer with baking paper and put the dumplings in the steamer in a single layer, seam side down, leaving a gap between each one.

4 Cover and steam the dumplings over a wok of simmering water for 8 minutes, or until cooked through.

Prawn toasts

»PREPARATION 20 MINUTES »COOKING TIME 15 MINUTES »MAKES 36

1 To make the sauce, combine the tomato sauce, garlic, chilli, hoisin sauce and worcestershire sauce in a bowl. Set aside until ready to serve.

2 Peel the prawns and gently pull out the dark vein from each prawn back, starting from the head end. Put the prawns in a food processor with the garlic, water chestnuts, coriander, ginger, egg whites, white pepper and ¼ teaspoon salt. Process for 20–30 seconds, or until smooth.

3 Brush the top of each slice of bread with lightly beaten egg yolk, then spread with the prawn mixture. Sprinkle generously with the sesame seeds, pressing down gently. Cut each slice of bread into three strips.

4 Fill a wok or deep heavy-based saucepan one-third full of oil and heat to 180°C (350°F/Gas 4), or until a cube of bread dropped into the oil browns in 15 seconds. Starting with the prawn mixture face down, deep-fry the toasts in small batches for 10–15 seconds, or until golden and crisp, turning over halfway through. Remove with tongs or a slotted spoon and drain on crumpled paper towel. Serve with the dipping sauce.

Dipping sauce

125 ml (4 fl oz/½ cup) tomato sauce (ketchup)
2 garlic cloves, crushed
2 small red chillies, seeded and finely chopped
2 tablespoons hoisin sauce
2 teaspoons worcestershire sauce

350 g (12 oz) raw prawns (shrimp)
1 garlic clove
75 g (2½ oz) tinned water chestnuts, drained
1 tablespoon chopped coriander (cilantro) leaves
2 cm (¾ inch) piece ginger, roughly chopped
2 eggs, separated
¼ teaspoon white pepper
12 slices white bread, crusts removed
155 g (5½ oz/1 cup) sesame seeds
oil, for deep-frying

Coconut prawns with chilli dressing

»PREPARATION 35 MINUTES + REFRIGERATION »COOKING TIME 30 MINUTES »SERVES 4

1 Peel the prawns and gently pull out the dark vein from each prawn back, starting from the head end. Holding the prawns by their tails, coat them in flour, then dip them into the combined egg and milk, and then in the combined shredded coconut and coriander. Refrigerate for 30 minutes.

2 To make the chilli dressing, heat the oil in a saucepan and cook the shallots, garlic, ginger, chilli and ground turmeric over medium heat for 3–5 minutes, or until fragrant. Add the coconut cream, makrut leaves, lime juice, sugar and fish sauce. Bring to the boil, reduce the heat and simmer for 2–3 minutes, or until thick. Keep warm.

3 Fill a wok or deep heavy-based saucepan one-third full of oil and heat to 180°C (350°F/Gas 4), or until a cube of bread dropped into the oil browns in 15 seconds. Holding the prawns by their tails, gently lower them into the wok and cook in batches for 3–5 minutes, or until golden. Drain on crumpled paper towel and season with salt.

4 Add the extra chopped coriander to the chilli dressing and serve with the prawns.

24 large raw prawns (shrimp)
plain (all-purpose) flour, to coat
1 egg
1 tablespoon milk
60 g (2¼ oz/1 cup) shredded coconut
1 handful coriander (cilantro) leaves, chopped
2½ tablespoons vegetable oil
300 g (10½ oz) red Asian shallots, chopped
2 garlic cloves, finely chopped
2 teaspoons finely chopped fresh ginger
1 red chilli, seeded and thinly sliced
1 teaspoon ground turmeric
270 ml (9½ fl oz) tinned coconut cream
2 makrut (kaffir lime) leaves, thinly sliced
2 teaspoons lime juice
2 teaspoons grated palm sugar (jaggery)
3 teaspoons fish sauce
oil, for deep-frying
1 tablespoon chopped coriander (cilantro) leaves, extra

Spinach and water chestnut dumplings

»PREPARATION 1 HOUR 30 MINUTES »COOKING TIME 50 MINUTES »MAKES 30

1 To make the dipping sauce, whisk the ingredients together in a small bowl and set aside.

2 To make the filling, add the oils to a wok over medium heat and swirl to coat the base and side. Stir-fry the garlic and ginger for 1 minute, or until fragrant but not brown. Add the garlic chives, water spinach, water chestnuts and soy sauce. Cook for 2 minutes, then remove from the wok and cool for about 5 minutes. Drain and discard any liquid.

3 To make the pastry, combine the rice flour, tapioca starch, arrowroot and rice flour in a large saucepan with 625 ml (21½ fl oz/2½ cups) water, stirring to remove any lumps. Stir over low heat for 10 minutes, or until thick. Cook, stirring, for a further 5 minutes, or until the liquid is opaque. Turn out onto a work surface dusted liberally with tapioca flour and cool for 10 minutes. (You will need to use the tapioca flour to continually dust the surface and your hands while kneading.) With floured hands, knead the dough for 10 minutes, or until smooth and elastic. Divide into two portions, covering one half with plastic wrap.

4 Roll out the dough until it is 2 mm (1/16 inch) thick. Cut 9 cm (3½ inch) rounds with a cutter. Place a heaped teaspoon of filling in the centre of each circle, dampen the edge with lukewarm water, fold over and pleat to seal. Place on a lightly floured board or tray and repeat with the remaining dough and filling. Do not re-roll the pastry scraps. Before steaming, lightly brush the dumplings with oil.

5 Line a bamboo steamer with lightly oiled baking paper. Put the dumplings in the steamer, leaving a gap between each one. Cover and steam in batches over a wok of simmering water for 10 minutes, or until the pastry is opaque. Serve the dumplings with the dipping sauce on the side.

Dipping sauce
½ teaspoon sesame oil
½ teaspoon peanut oil
1 tablespoon soy sauce
1 tablespoon lime juice
1 small red chilli, seeded and
  finely chopped

Filling
1 tablespoon peanut oil
1 teaspoon sesame oil
1 garlic clove, crushed
2.5 cm (1 inch) piece fresh ginger,
  grated
2 tablespoons chopped garlic chives
30 g (1 oz) water spinach (ong choy),
  chopped into 1 cm (½ inch) lengths
120 g (4¼ oz) tinned water chestnuts,
  drained, then finely chopped
1 tablespoon soy sauce

Pastry
350 g (12 oz/2 cups) rice flour
85 g (3 oz/⅔ cup) tapioca starch
2 tablespoons arrowroot flour
1 tablespoon glutinous rice flour
tapioca flour, for dusting
oil, for brushing

Gyoza

» PREPARATION 50 MINUTES » COOKING TIME 25 MINUTES » MAKES 40

1 Put the Chinese cabbage and ½ teaspoon salt in a colander, then sit the colander in a large bowl. Toss to combine and then leave to drain for 30 minutes, stirring occasionally. This process will draw out the liquid from the cabbage and prevent the filling from going soggy.

2 Put the pork, garlic, ginger, spring onion, cornflour, soy sauce, rice wine and sesame oil in a bowl and mix with your hands.

3 Rinse the cabbage under cold running water. Press dry between layers of paper towel. Add to the pork mixture and combine well.

4 Place 1 teaspoon of the pork mixture in the centre of each dumpling wrapper and brush the inside edge with a little water. Bring the two edges of the wrapper together to form a semi-circle. Using your thumb and index finger, create a pleat, pressing firmly and gently tapping the gyoza on a work surface to form a flat bottom. Repeat to make 40 gyoza.

5 Heat a quarter of the oil in a wok over medium–high heat. Cook the gyoza in batches for 2 minutes, flat side down. Reduce the heat and add a quarter of the stock, shaking the wok gently to unstick the gyoza. Cover and steam for 4 minutes, or until the liquid has evaporated. Remove and keep warm. Repeat with the remaining oil, gyoza and stock. Serve with the soy sauce or Chinese black vinegar, for dipping.

150 g (5½ oz) Chinese cabbage (wong bok), finely shredded
225 g (8 oz) minced (ground) pork
2 garlic cloves, finely chopped
2 teaspoons finely chopped fresh ginger
2 spring onions (scallions), finely chopped
2 teaspoons cornflour (cornstarch)
1 tablespoon light soy sauce
2 teaspoons Chinese rice wine
2 teaspoons sesame oil
40 round Shanghai dumpling wrappers
2 tablespoons vegetable oil
125 ml (4 fl oz/½ cup) chicken stock
soy sauce or Chinese black vinegar, to serve

Noodle nests with smoked salmon tartare

»PREPARATION 25 MINUTES »COOKING TIME 20 MINUTES »MAKES 30

1 Preheat the oven to 200°C (400°F/ Gas 6). Lightly grease three 12-hole mini-muffin tins. (You can use two 12-hole mini-muffin tins and cook the remaining six after the first batch is finished.) Use scissors or a sharp knife to cut the noodles into 10 cm (4 inch) lengths. Put the noodles in a heatproof bowl and pour boiling water over to cover. Soak for 5 minutes, then drain and pat dry with paper towels. Divide the noodles among 30 holes of the mini-muffin tins, pressing down to form 'nests'. Brush lightly with olive oil and bake for 15 minutes.

2 Turn out the noodles onto a wire rack, then put the rack in the oven for 5 minutes, or until the noodles are crisp.

3 Stir together the salmon, extra virgin olive oil, vinegar, mayonnaise, garlic and chopped dill. Spoon a heaped teaspoon into each noodle nest and garnish with dill.

200 g (7 oz) fresh flat egg noodles
olive oil, for brushing
200 g (7 oz) smoked salmon, diced
1 tablespoon extra virgin olive oil
3 teaspoons white wine vinegar
125 g (4½ oz/½ cup) whole-egg
   mayonnaise
1 garlic clove, crushed
1 tablespoon finely chopped dill
dill sprigs, to garnish

Chilli puffs with curried vegetables

»PREPARATION 35 MINUTES »COOKING TIME 1 HOUR 5 MINUTES »MAKES 12

1 Preheat the oven to 210°C (415°F/ Gas 6–7). Sprinkle two 28 x 32 cm (11¼ x 12¾ inch) baking trays with a little water.

2 To make the choux pastry, put the butter in a saucepan with 310 ml (10¾ fl oz/1¼ cups) water. Stir over low heat for 5 minutes, or until the butter melts and the mixture comes to the boil. Remove from the heat, add the flour and chilli powder all at once and stir with a wooden spoon until just combined.

3 Return the pan to the heat and beat constantly over low heat for 3 minutes, or until the mixture thickens and comes away from the side and base of the pan. Transfer the mixture to a large bowl. Using electric beaters, beat the mixture on high speed for 1 minute. Add the egg gradually, beating until the mixture is stiff and glossy. (This stage could take up to 5 minutes.)

4 Spoon the pastry mixture onto the prepared trays in 12 mounds, spacing them 10 cm (4 inches) apart. Sprinkle with a little water and bake for 20 minutes. Reduce the heat to 180°C (350°F/Gas 4). Bake for another 50 minutes, or until the puffs are crisp and well browned. (Cut a slit into each puff halfway through cooking to allow any excess steam to escape and the puff to dry out.) Transfer the puffs to a wire rack to cool.

5 For the curried vegetables, thinly slice the squash. Cut the snow peas in half diagonally. Cut the carrot into thin strips and slice the onions. Heat the butter in a frying pan and add the onions. Cook over low heat for 5 minutes, or until golden, then stir in the curry paste. Add the oyster mushrooms and the other vegetables and stir over high heat for 1 minute. Add the lemon juice, remove from the heat and stir. Cut the puffs in half and remove any uncooked mixture from the centre with a spoon. Fill the puffs with the vegetables and serve immediately.

Choux pastry
90 g (3¼ oz) butter
155 g (5½ oz/1¼ cups) plain (all-purpose) flour, sifted
¼ teaspoon chilli powder
4 eggs, lightly beaten

Curried vegetables
4 yellow squash
100 g (3½ oz) snow peas (mangetout)
1 carrot
2 onions
50 g (1¾ oz) butter
2 tablespoons mild curry paste
300 g (10½ oz) small oyster mushrooms
1 tablespoon lemon juice

Bondas

»PREPARATION 30 MINUTES »COOKING TIME 25 MINUTES »MAKES 24

1 Heat a wok over medium heat. Add the oil and swirl to coat the base and side. Add the mustard seeds and stir for 30 seconds, or until fragrant. Add the onion, ginger, curry leaves and chilli and cook for 2 minutes. Add the diced potato, turmeric and 2 teaspoons water and stir for 2 minutes, until the mixture is dry. Remove the pan from the heat and cool. Stir in the lemon juice and coriander, then season to taste. Shape into 24 balls, using 1 heaped tablespoon of the mixture for each ball.

2 To make the batter, sift the flours, ground turmeric, chilli powder and ¼ teaspoon salt into a bowl. Make a well in the centre. Gradually whisk in 330 ml (11¼ fl oz/1⅓ cups) water to make a smooth batter.

3 Fill a wok one-third full of oil and heat to 180°C (350°F/Gas 4), or until a cube of bread dropped into the oil browns in 15 seconds. Dip the balls into the batter, then cook in the hot oil, in batches, for 1–2 minutes, or until golden. Drain on crumpled paper towel and season with salt. Serve hot.

2 teaspoons vegetable oil
1 teaspoon brown mustard seeds
1 onion, finely chopped
2 teaspoons grated fresh ginger
4 curry leaves
3 small green chillies, finely chopped
1.25 kg (2 lb 12 oz) all-purpose potatoes, diced and cooked
pinch ground turmeric
2 tablespoons lemon juice
20 g (¾ oz) chopped coriander (cilantro) leaves
oil, for deep-frying

Batter
110 g (3¾ oz/1 cup) besan (chickpea flour)
30 g (1 oz/¼ cup) self-raising flour
45 g (1¾ oz/¼ cup) rice flour
¼ teaspoon ground turmeric
1 teaspoon chilli powder

Indian dal with pitta toasts

»PREPARATION 15 MINUTES   »COOKING TIME 1 HOUR 25 MINUTES   »SERVES 4–6

1 Put the red lentils in a large bowl and cover with water. Remove any floating particles and drain the lentils well.

2 Finely chop the onion. Heat the ghee in a saucepan. Fry the onion for about 3 minutes, or until soft. Add the garlic, ginger and spices and cook, stirring, for 1 minute.

3 Add the red lentils and 500 ml (17 fl oz/2 cups) water and bring to the boil. Reduce the heat and simmer, stirring occasionally, for 15 minutes, or until the water has been absorbed. Watch carefully towards the end of cooking time, as the mixture could burn on the bottom of the pan.

4 Meanwhile, to make the pitta toasts, preheat the oven to 180°C (350°F/Gas 4). Cut the pitta bread into wedges and brush lightly with the oil. Arrange on a baking tray and cook for 5–7 minutes, or until lightly browned and crisp.

5 Transfer the dal to a serving bowl. Serve warm or at room temperature with the pitta toasts or with naan or pitta bread.

Note Oil may be used instead of the ghee if ghee is difficult to obtain. You can also make your own ghee. Melt some butter, skim away the white froth on the surface and then pour the clear butter into another container, leaving all of the white residue behind.

310 g (11 oz/1¼ cups) red lentils
1 onion
2 tablespoons ghee (see Note)
2 garlic cloves, crushed
1 teaspoon grated fresh ginger
1 teaspoon ground turmeric
1 teaspoon garam masala

Pitta toasts
4 pitta bread rounds
2–3 tablespoons olive oil

Pork and lemon grass won tons

» PREPARATION 35 MINUTES + REFRIGERATION » COOKING TIME 35 MINUTES » MAKES 56

1 Put the pork, ginger, lemon grass, water chestnuts, garlic chives, chilli paste, plum sauce, chilli oil, sesame oil and cornflour in a bowl and mix with your hands until combined. Cover, then refrigerate for 1 hour.

2 To make the dipping sauce, combine the ingredients in a jar with a lid and shake to combine. Refrigerate until needed.

3 Work with one won ton wrapper at a time, keeping the rest covered. Spoon 2 teaspoons of the filling into the centre of the wrapper and lightly brush the edges with water. Gather up the corners, bring them together in the centre and press firmly to seal. Repeat with the remaining wrappers and filling.

4 Fill a wok or deep heavy-based saucepan one-third full of oil and heat to 180°C (350°F/Gas 4), or until a cube of bread dropped into the oil browns in 15 seconds. Deep-fry the won tons in batches for about 3–4 minutes, until lightly browned. Remove with a slotted spoon, drain on crumpled paper towel and serve hot with the dipping sauce.

400 g (14 oz) minced (ground) pork
1 teaspoon finely chopped fresh ginger
1 lemon grass stem, white part only, finely sliced
230 g (8 oz) tinned water chestnuts, drained and finely chopped
2 tablespoons finely chopped garlic chives
½ teaspoon chilli paste
2 tablespoons plum sauce
1 teaspoon chilli oil
1 teaspoon sesame oil
1 tablespoon cornflour (cornstarch)
56 square won ton wrappers
oil, for deep-frying

Dipping sauce
125 ml (4 fl oz/½ cup) light soy sauce
60 ml (2 fl oz/¼ cup) balsamic vinegar
1 teaspoon finely grated fresh ginger
1 teaspoon chilli oil

Layered sushi

»PREPARATION 25 MINUTES + REFRIGERATION »COOKING TIME 35 MINUTES »MAKES 36

1 Wash the rice in a strainer under cold running water until the water runs clear, then leave in the strainer to drain for an hour. Put the rice in a saucepan with 750 ml (26 fl oz/ 3 cups) water and bring to the boil. Cook for 5–10 minutes, or until tunnels form on the surface of the rice. Reduce the heat to low, cover and cook for 12–15 minutes, or until the rice is cooked and all the water has been absorbed. Remove from the heat, remove the lid from the pan, cover the rice with a clean tea towel (dish towel) and leave for 15 minutes.

2 Combine the vinegar, mirin, sugar and 1 teaspoon salt in a small bowl and stir until the sugar has dissolved. Spread the rice over the base of a non-metallic dish or bowl, pour the vinegar mixture over the top and use a spatula or rice paddle to mix the dressing through the rice, separating the grains — the aim is to make the rice grains stick together slightly. Fan the rice until it cools to room temperature.

3 Combine the mayonnaise and wasabi in a small bowl. Lay a sheet of nori, shiny side up, on top of a piece of baking paper on a dry tray. Entirely cover the nori with a cup of loosely packed rice. Spread with a little wasabi mayonnaise, then top with a layer of smoked salmon and some slices of pickled ginger. Place another sheet of nori on top and flatten lightly with a rolling pin. Repeat the layering twice, to form three layers, finishing with a sheet of nori, and again flattening with the rolling pin. Reserve the rest of the wasabi mayonnaise.

4 Cover and refrigerate the sushi for at least an hour, then, using a very sharp knife dipped in water, trim any filling protruding from the edges and slice into 2 cm (¾ inch) squares. Garnish the squares with wasabi mayonnaise, pickled ginger and black sesame seeds.

550 g (1 lb 4 oz/2½ cups) Japanese short-grain rice
100 ml (3½ fl oz) rice vinegar
1 tablespoon mirin
55 g (2 oz/¼ cup) caster (superfine) sugar
90 g (3¼ oz/⅓ cup) Japanese mayonnaise
2 teaspoons wasabi paste
4 sheets roasted nori
300 g (10½ oz) smoked salmon
40 g (1½ oz/¼ cup) pickled ginger slices, to garnish
black sesame seeds, to garnish

Vegetable dumplings

» PREPARATION 40 MINUTES » COOKING TIME 20 MINUTES » MAKES 24

1 Soak the shiitake mushrooms in boiling water for 20 minutes. Squeeze dry, discard the stems and finely chop the caps.

2 Heat a wok over high heat, add the oil and swirl to coat. Stir-fry the ginger, garlic, white pepper and a pinch of salt for 30 seconds. Add the chives and water spinach and cook for 1 minute. Combine the stock, oyster sauce, cornflour, soy sauce and rice wine. Add to wok with the water chestnuts and mushrooms. Cook for 1–2 minutes, until it has thickened, then remove from the heat and cool completely.

3 To make the wrappers, combine the wheat starch and cornflour in a bowl. Make a well in the centre and add the boiling water, a little at a time, bringing the mixture together with your hands. When the dough is combined, immediately knead using lightly oiled hands until it forms a shiny ball.

4 Keeping the dough covered with a cloth while you work, pick walnut-sized pieces from the dough and, using well-oiled hands, squash them between the palms of your hands. Roll the pieces out as thinly as possible into rounds no larger than 10 cm (4 inches) in diameter. Place 1 tablespoon of filling in the centre of each round. Pinch the edges of the wrapper together to enclose the filling and form a tight ball.

5 Place the dumplings in a single layer in a bamboo steamer lined with baking paper, leaving a gap between each one. Cover and steam each batch over a wok of simmering water for 7–8 minutes. Serve with chilli sauce.

Note Wheat starch is a very fine white powder similar to cornflour (cornstarch) in texture. It is available at Asian grocery stores.

8 dried shiitake mushrooms
1 tablespoon vegetable oil
2 teaspoons finely chopped fresh ginger
2 garlic cloves, crushed
pinch white pepper
100 g (3½ oz/1½ cups) garlic chives, chopped
100 g (3½ oz) water spinach (ong choy), cut into 1 cm (½ inch) lengths
60 ml (2 fl oz/¼ cup) chicken stock
2 tablespoons oyster sauce
1 tablespoon cornflour (cornstarch)
1 teaspoon soy sauce
1 teaspoon Chinese rice wine
45 g (1½ oz/¼ cup) tinned water chestnuts, chopped
chilli sauce, to serve

Wrappers
200 g (7 oz) wheat starch (see Note)
1 teaspoon cornflour (cornstarch)
185 ml (6 fl oz/¾ cup) boiling water
oil, for kneading

Peking duck with mandarin pancakes

»PREPARATION 1 HOUR + 4 HOURS DRYING »COOKING TIME 1 HOUR 15 MINUTES »SERVES 6

1 Remove the neck and any large pieces of fat from inside the duck. Hold the duck over the sink and very carefully and slowly pour the boiling water over the duck, rotating it so the water scalds all the skin. Place the duck on a wire rack in an ovenproof dish. Mix the honey and 125 ml (4 fl oz/½ cup) hot water and brush two coats of this glaze over the duck. Dry the duck in a cool, airy place for about 4 hours. The skin is sufficiently dry when it feels papery.

2 Preheat the oven to 210°C (415°F/ Gas 6–7). Cut a section from the white end of each spring onion, about 8 cm (3¼ inch) long. Make fine parallel cuts from the top of the section towards the white end. Put the onion pieces in iced water — they will open into 'brushes'.

3 Roast the duck for 30 minutes, then turn it over carefully without tearing the skin and roast it for another 30 minutes. Remove the duck from the oven and leave for a minute or two, then place on a warm dish.

4 Meanwhile, for the pancakes, put the flour and sugar in a bowl and pour in the boiling water. Stir the mixture a few times and leave until lukewarm. Knead the mixture, on a lightly floured surface, into a smooth dough. Cover and set aside for 30 minutes. Take two level tablespoons of dough and roll each one into a ball. Roll out to circles 8 cm (3¼ inches) in diameter. Lightly brush one of the circles with sesame oil and place the other circle on top. Re-roll the dough to make a thin pancake about 15 cm (6 inches) in diameter. Repeat with the rest of the dough and oil to make about 10 'double' pancakes.

5 Heat a frying pan and cook the pancakes one at a time. When small bubbles appear on the surface, turn the pancake over and cook the second side, pressing the surface with a clean tea towel (dish towel). The pancake should puff up when done. Transfer the pancake to a plate. When cool enough to handle, peel the two halves of the double pancake apart. Stack them on a plate and cover them at once to prevent them drying out.

6 To serve, thinly slice the duck. Place the pancakes and duck on separate serving plates. Arrange the cucumber sticks and spring onion brushes on another serving plate. Put the hoisin sauce in a small dish. Each diner helps themselves to a pancake, spreads a little sauce on it and adds a couple of pieces of cucumber, a spring onion brush and, finally, a piece of duck. The pancake is then folded over into a neat envelope for eating.

1.7 kg (3 lb 12 oz) duck, washed
3 litres (104 fl oz/12 cups) boiling water
1 tablespoon honey
12 spring onions (scallions)
1 Lebanese (short) cucumber, seeded and cut into batons
2 tablespoons hoisin sauce

Mandarin pancakes
310 g (11 oz/2½ cups) plain (all-purpose) flour
2 teaspoons caster (superfine) sugar
250 ml (9 fl oz/1 cup) boiling water
1 tablespoon sesame oil

Vegetable pakoras

» PREPARATION 30 MINUTES » COOKING TIME 20 MINUTES » SERVES 4

1 To make the raita, mix the cucumber and yoghurt in a bowl. Dry-fry the cumin and mustard seeds in a small frying pan over medium heat for 1 minute, or until fragrant and lightly browned, then add to the yoghurt mixture. Stir in the ginger, season to taste and mix together well. Garnish with paprika. Refrigerate until ready to serve.

2 Sift the besan, self-raising and soy flours into a bowl, then add the turmeric, cayenne pepper, ground coriander, chilli and 1 teaspoon salt. Gradually whisk in 250 ml (9 fl oz/ 1 cup) cold water to form a batter. Set aside for 15 minutes. Preheat the oven to 120°C (235°F/Gas ½).

3 Meanwhile, cut the cauliflower into small florets. Cut the sweet potato and eggplant into 5 mm (¼ inch) slices. Cut the asparagus into 6 cm (2½ inch) lengths.

4 Fill a wok one-third full with oil and heat to 170°C (325°F/Gas 3), or until a cube of bread dropped into the oil browns in 15 seconds. Dip the vegetables into the batter, then deep-fry them in small batches, for 1–2 minutes, or until pale golden. Remove with a slotted spoon and drain on crumpled paper towel. Keep warm in the oven until all the vegetables are cooked. Serve with the raita.

Raita
2 Lebanese (short) cucumbers, peeled, seeded and finely chopped
250 g (9 oz/1 cup) plain yoghurt
1 teaspoon ground cumin
1 teaspoon mustard seeds
½ teaspoon grated fresh ginger
paprika, to garnish

35 g (1¼ oz/⅓ cup) besan (chickpea flour)
40 g (1½ oz/⅓ cup) self-raising flour
45 g (1¾ oz/⅓ cup) soy flour
½ teaspoon ground turmeric
1 teaspoon cayenne pepper
½ teaspoon ground coriander
1 small green chilli, seeded and finely chopped
200 g (7 oz) cauliflower
140 g (5 oz) orange sweet potato
180 g (6¼ oz) eggplant (aubergine)
180 g (6¼ oz) asparagus, woody ends trimmed
oil, for deep-frying

Pork and noodle balls with sweet chilli sauce

»PREPARATION 30 MINUTES »COOKING TIME 15 MINUTES »MAKES 30

1 To make the dipping sauce, combine the sweet chilli sauce, mirin, ginger and Japanese soy sauce in a bowl. Set aside.

2 Place the noodles in a bowl and cover with boiling water. Soak for about 1 minute, or until tender. Drain very well and pat dry with paper towel. Cut the noodles into 5 cm (2 inch) lengths, then transfer to a bowl. Add the pork, spring onion, garlic, coriander, fish sauce, oyster sauce and lime juice and combine the mixture well using your hands, making sure the pork is evenly distributed.

3 Using a tablespoon of mixture at a time, roll each spoonful into a ball to make 30 in total, shaping and pressing each ball firmly with your hands to ensure they remain intact.

4 Fill a wok or deep heavy-based saucepan one-third full of oil and heat to 180°C (350°F/Gas 4), or until a cube of bread dropped into the oil browns in 15 seconds. Deep-fry the balls in batches for 2–3 minutes, or until golden and cooked through. Drain on crumpled paper towel. Serve hot with dipping sauce.

Dipping sauce
80 ml (2½ fl oz/⅓ cup) sweet chilli sauce
2 teaspoons mirin
2 teaspoons finely chopped fresh ginger
125 ml (4 fl oz/½ cup) Japanese soy sauce

250 g (9 oz) hokkien (egg) noodles
300 g (10½ oz) minced (ground) pork
6 spring onions (scallions), finely chopped
2 garlic cloves, crushed
4 tablespoons finely chopped coriander (cilantro) leaves
1 tablespoon fish sauce
2 tablespoons oyster sauce
1½ tablespoons lime juice
peanut oil, for deep-frying

35 Phad Thai

38 Vietnamese crepes

40 General Tso's chicken

45 Pork noodle salad

47 Yoghurt rice

Noodles,
rice and stir-fry

Tofu in black bean sauce

»PREPARATION 20 MINUTES »COOKING TIME 15 MINUTES »SERVES 4

1 Cut the red capsicum in half, remove the seeds and membrane and cut into 2 cm (¾ inch) chunks. Cut the tofu into 2 cm (¾ inch) cubes and chop the baby bok choy, crossways, into 2 cm (¾ inch) pieces. Finely chop the black beans. Slice the spring onions on the diagonal, including some green.

2 Combine the stock, cornflour, Chinese rice wine, sesame oil, soy sauce, ½ teaspoon salt and some freshly ground black pepper.

3 Heat a wok over medium heat, add the peanut oil and swirl to coat the base and side. Add the tofu and stir-fry in two batches for 3 minutes each batch, or until lightly browned.

Remove with a slotted spoon and drain on paper towel. Discard any bits of tofu that are stuck to the wok or floating in the oil.

4 Add the garlic and ginger and stir-fry for 30 seconds. Toss in the black beans and spring onion and stir-fry for 30 seconds. Add the red capsicum and stir-fry for 1 minute. Add the baby bok choy and stir-fry for 2 minutes. Return the tofu to the wok and stir gently. Add the sauce. Stir gently for 2–3 minutes, or until the sauce has thickened slightly. Serve immediately with steamed rice.

1 red capsicum (pepper)
450 g (1 lb) firm tofu
300 g (10½ oz) baby bok choy (pak choy)
50 g (1¾ oz/¼ cup) black beans, rinsed
4 spring onions (scallions)
80 ml (2½ fl oz/⅓ cup) vegetable stock
2 teaspoons cornflour (cornstarch)
2 teaspoons Chinese rice wine
1 teaspoon sesame oil
1 tablespoon soy sauce
2 tablespoons peanut oil
2 garlic cloves, very finely chopped
2 teaspoons finely chopped fresh ginger

Phad Thai

»PREPARATION 25 MINUTES   »COOKING TIME 10 MINUTES   »SERVES 4–6

1 Put the noodles in a heatproof bowl, cover with warm water and soak for 15–20 minutes, or until soft and pliable. Drain well.

2 Combine the tamarind purée with 1 tablespoon water. Put the chilli, garlic and spring onion in a spice grinder or mortar and pestle and grind to a smooth paste. Transfer the mixture to a bowl. Stir in the tamarind mixture along with the sugar, fish sauce and lime juice, stirring until combined.

3 Heat a wok until very hot, add 1 tablespoon of the oil and swirl to coat. Add the egg, swirl to coat and cook for 1–2 minutes, or until set. Remove, roll up and slice thinly.

4 Peel the prawns and gently pull out the dark vein from each prawn back, starting from the head end.

5 Heat the remaining oil in the wok, stir in the chilli mixture and stir-fry for 30 seconds. Add the pork and stir-fry for 2 minutes, or until tender. Add the prawns and stir-fry for 1 minute, or until pink and curled.

6 Stir in the noodles, egg strips, tofu and bean sprouts and gently toss everything together until heated through. Serve immediately, topped with the peanuts, coriander and lime wedges.

250 g (9 oz) dried rice stick noodles
1 tablespoon tamarind purée
1 small red chilli, chopped
2 garlic cloves, chopped
2 spring onions (scallions), sliced
1½ tablespoons sugar
2 tablespoons fish sauce
2 tablespoons lime juice
2 tablespoons oil
2 eggs, beaten
8 large raw prawns (shrimp)
150 g (5½ oz) pork fillet, thinly sliced
100 g (3½ oz) fried tofu puffs, cut into thin strips
90 g (3¼ oz/1 cup) bean sprouts
40 g (1½ oz/¼ cup) chopped roasted peanuts
3 tablespoons coriander (cilantro) leaves
1 lime, cut into wedges

Asian greens with teriyaki tofu dressing

»PREPARATION 15 MINUTES »COOKING TIME 20 MINUTES »SERVES 6

1 Cut the baby bok choy and choy sum widthways into thirds. Cut the snake beans into 10 cm (4 inch) lengths. Thinly slice onion. Heat a wok over high heat, add 1 tablespoon of oil and swirl to coat the base and side. Cook onion for 3-5 minutes, or until crisp. Remove with a slotted spoon and drain on paper towel.

2 Reheat the wok over high heat and add 1 tablespoon of oil. Add half the greens and stir-fry for 2–3 minutes, or until wilted. Remove from wok. Repeat with remaining oil and greens. Drain any liquid from the wok.

3 Add the combined sugar, chilli powder, ginger and teriyaki sauce to the wok, then bring to the boil. Simmer for 1 minute. Add the sesame oil and tofu and simmer for 2 minutes, turning once — the tofu will break up. Divide the greens among six serving plates, then top with the dressing. Sprinkle with the fried onion.

650 g (1 lb 7 oz) baby bok choy (pak choy)

500 g (1 lb 2 oz) choy sum

440 g (15½ oz) snake (yard-long) beans, topped and tailed

1 onion

60 ml (2 fl oz/¼ cup) vegetable oil

60 g (2¼ oz/⅓ cup) soft brown sugar

½ teaspoon chilli powder

2 tablespoons grated fresh ginger

250 ml (9 fl oz/1 cup) teriyaki sauce

1 tablespoon sesame oil

600 g (1 lb 5 oz) silken firm tofu, drained

Spring onion lamb

1 Combine the rice wine with 1 tablespoon of the soy sauce, the white pepper and ½ teaspoon salt in a large non-metallic bowl. Add the lamb and toss well to coat in the marinade. Cover with plastic wrap and marinate in the refrigerator for at least 10 minutes.

2 To make the sauce, combine the vinegar, sesame oil and 1 tablespoon soy sauce in a small non-metallic bowl. Set aside until needed.

3 Heat a wok over high heat, add 2 teaspoons of the vegetable oil and swirl to coat the base and side. Add the choy sum, stir-fry briefly, then add a third of the crushed garlic and the remaining soy sauce. Cook for 3 minutes, or until cooked, but still crisp. Remove from the wok and keep warm.

4 Wipe the wok with paper towel, then reheat the wok over high heat. Add 1 tablespoon of the vegetable oil and swirl to coat the base and side. Stir-fry the marinated lamb over high heat in two batches for 1–2 minutes, or until browned. Remove from the wok.

5 Add a little more oil to the wok if necessary, then add the spring onion and remaining garlic and stir-fry for 1–2 minutes. Pour the prepared sauce into the wok and stir for 1 minute, until combined. Return the lamb to the wok and stir-fry for a further minute, until combined and heated through. Serve the lamb immediately with the choy sum.

1 tablespoon Chinese rice wine
60 ml (2 fl oz/¼ cup) soy sauce
½ teaspoon white pepper
600 g (1 lb 5 oz) lean lamb loin fillets, thinly sliced across the grain
1 tablespoon Chinese black vinegar
1 teaspoon sesame oil
2 tablespoons vegetable oil
750 g (1 lb 10 oz) choy sum, cut into 10 cm (4 inch) lengths
3 garlic cloves, crushed
6 spring onions (scallions), cut into 10 cm (4 inch) lengths

Vietnamese crepes
with pork, prawns and noodles

»PREPARATION 45 MINUTES + STANDING »COOKING TIME 35 MINUTES »SERVES 6

1 To make the crepe batter, blend the rice flour, baking powder, sugar, turmeric, coconut milk, ½ teaspoon salt and 250 ml (9 fl oz/1 cup) water in a blender to a smooth batter. Cover and leave in a warm place for 2–4 hours.

2 Mix together the dipping sauce ingredients in a small bowl. Toss all the salad ingredients together in a large bowl.

3 To make the filling, peel the prawns and gently pull out the dark vein from each prawn back, starting at the head end. Roughly chop the prawn meat. Remove the seeds and membrane from the red capsicum and then thinly slice the capsicum, mushrooms and spring onions. Break the vermicelli noodles into pieces and soak in boiling water for 6–7 minutes, until soft. Drain. Heat a wok over high heat, add the oil and swirl to coat. Stir-fry the onion for 2 minutes, then add the garlic and cook for a further 30 seconds. Add the minced pork and cook for 2 minutes, or until browned. Stir in

the chopped prawns, capsicum and mushrooms. Cook until the prawns change colour. Stir in the noodles, soy sauce, white pepper and sliced spring onion.

4 Heat ½ teaspoon of the peanut oil in a 30 cm (12 inch) non-stick frying pan. Whisk the crepe batter until smooth. Pour 80 ml (2½ fl oz/⅓ cup) of the batter into the centre of the pan, and swirl to spread to the edges. Cook over medium heat for 1–2 minutes, until golden and crispy. Turn and repeat on the other side. Repeat with the remaining oil and batter to make six crepes.

5 To assemble, place a portion of filling on half of each crepe and fold the other side over. Serve with the sauce, salad and lime wedges.

290 g (10¼ oz/1⅔ cups) rice flour
1 teaspoon baking powder
1½ teaspoons sugar
½ teaspoon ground turmeric
250 ml (9 fl oz/1 cup) coconut milk
3 teaspoons peanut oil
lime wedges, to serve

Dipping sauce
2 tablespoons lime juice
1 tablespoon fish sauce
1 tablespoon caster (superfine) sugar
1 small red chilli, finely chopped

Salad
1 carrot, roughly grated
120 g (4¼ oz) iceberg lettuce, shredded
1 Lebanese (short) cucumber, cut into thin batons
100 g (3½ oz) bean sprouts, trimmed
2 large handfuls mint
2 large handfuls coriander (cilantro) leaves

Filling
250 g (9 oz) raw prawns (shrimp)
1 small red capsicum (pepper)
80 g (2¾ oz) button mushrooms
4 spring onions (scallions)
80 g (2¾ oz) dried rice vermicelli
1 tablespoon peanut oil
1 large onion, thinly sliced
6 garlic cloves, crushed
200 g (7 oz) lean minced (ground) pork fillet
1 tablespoon light soy sauce
¼ teaspoon ground white pepper

General Tso's chicken

»PREPARATION 15 MINUTES + MARINATING »COOKING TIME 10 MINUTES »SERVES 4–6

1 Combine the rice wine, cornflour, 2 tablespoons of the soy sauce and 2 teaspoons of the sesame oil in a large non-metallic bowl. Add the chicken and toss to coat, then cover and marinate in the refrigerator for 1 hour.

2 Meanwhile, soak the dried citrus peel in warm water for 20 minutes. Remove from the water and finely chop — you will need 1½ teaspoons chopped peel.

3 Heat the peanut oil in a wok over high heat. Drain the chicken from the marinade, then add to the wok in batches and stir-fry for 2 minutes at a time, or until browned and just cooked through. Remove from the oil with a slotted spoon and leave to drain in a colander or sieve.

4 Drain all but 1 tablespoon of the oil from the wok. Reheat the wok over high heat, then add the chilli flakes and ginger and stir-fry for 10 seconds. Return all the chicken to the wok, along with the spring onion, sugar, citrus peel, remaining soy sauce and sesame oil, and ½ teaspoon salt, and stir-fry for a further 2–3 minutes, or until well combined and warmed through. Garnish with the extra spring onion and serve with steamed rice.

Note This dish is named after a 19th-century Chinese general from Yunnan province.

2 tablespoons Chinese rice wine
1 tablespoon cornflour (cornstarch)
80 ml (2½ fl oz/⅓ cup) dark soy sauce
3 teaspoons sesame oil
900 g (2 lb) boneless, skinless chicken thighs, cut into 3 cm (1¼ inch) cubes
2 pieces dried citrus peel
125 ml (4 fl oz/½ cup) peanut oil
1½–2 teaspoons chilli flakes
2 tablespoons finely chopped fresh ginger
60 g (2¼ oz/1 cup) thinly sliced spring onions (scallions), plus extra, to garnish
2 teaspoons sugar
steamed rice, to serve

Cantonese lemon chicken

»PREPARATION 15 MINUTES »COOKING TIME 25 MINUTES »SERVES 4

1 Cut the chicken into strips, about 1 cm (½ inch) wide, then set aside. Combine the egg with 1 tablespoon of water, the soy sauce, sherry and cornflour in a small bowl and mix until smooth. Pour the egg mixture over the chicken, mixing well, and set aside for 10 minutes.

2 Sift the extra cornflour and plain flour together onto a plate. Roll each piece of chicken in the flour, coating each piece evenly, and shake off the excess. Place the chicken in a single layer on a plate.

3 Fill a wok one-third full of oil and heat to 180°C (350°F/Gas 4), or until a cube of bread dropped into the oil browns in 15 seconds. Carefully lower the chicken pieces into the oil, in batches, and cook for 2 minutes, or until golden brown. Remove the chicken with a slotted spoon and drain on paper towel. Repeat with the remaining chicken. Set aside while preparing the sauce. Reserve the oil in the wok.

4 To make the lemon sauce, combine 2 tablespoons of water, the lemon juice, sugar and sherry in a small saucepan. Bring to the boil over medium heat, stirring until the sugar dissolves. Stir the cornflour into 1 tablespoon water and mix to a smooth paste, then add to the lemon juice mixture, stirring until the sauce boils and thickens, then remove from the heat.

5 Just before serving, reheat the oil in the wok to very hot, add all the chicken pieces and deep-fry for 2 minutes, or until very crisp and a rich golden brown. Remove the chicken with a slotted spoon and drain well on paper towel. Pile the chicken onto a serving plate, drizzle over the sauce, sprinkle with spring onion and serve immediately.

Note The first deep-frying of the chicken pieces can be done several hours in advance.

500 g (1 lb 2 oz) boneless, skinless chicken breasts
1 egg yolk, lightly beaten
2 teaspoons soy sauce
2 teaspoons dry sherry
3 teaspoons cornflour (cornstarch)
60 g (2¼ oz/½ cup) cornflour (cornstarch), extra
2½ tablespoons plain (all-purpose) flour
oil, for deep-frying
4 spring onions (scallions), thinly sliced

Lemon sauce
80 ml (2½ fl oz/⅓ cup) lemon juice
2 tablespoons sugar
1 tablespoon dry sherry
2 teaspoons cornflour (cornstarch)

Seared scallops with chilli bean paste

»PREPARATION 20 MINUTES »COOKING TIME 15 MINUTES »SERVES 4

1 Put the noodles in a heatproof bowl, cover with boiling water and soak for 1 minute to separate them. Drain and rinse, then drain again. Set aside.

2 Heat a wok over high heat, add 2 tablespoons peanut oil and swirl to coat. Add the scallops in batches and sear for 20 seconds on each side, or until sealed. Remove from the wok and set aside.

3 Heat the remaining peanut oil in the wok and stir-fry the onion for 1–2 minutes, or until softened. Add the garlic and ginger and cook for 30 seconds. Stir in the chilli bean paste and cook for 1 minute, or until fragrant. Add the choy sum, noodles, chicken stock, soy sauce and kecap manis, and stir-fry for 4 minutes, or until the choy sum has wilted and the noodles have absorbed most of the liquid. Return all of the scallops to the wok, add the coriander, bean sprouts, chilli, sesame oil and rice wine, tossing gently until combined. Serve the scallops immediately.

500 g (1 lb 2 oz) hokkien (egg) noodles
60 ml (2 fl oz/¼ cup) peanut oil
20 scallops, roe removed
1 large onion, cut into thin wedges
3 garlic cloves, crushed
1 tablespoon grated fresh ginger
1 tablespoon chilli bean paste
150 g (5½ oz) choy sum, cut into 5 cm (2 inch) lengths
60 ml (2 fl oz/¼ cup) chicken stock
2 tablespoons light soy sauce
2 tablespoons kecap manis
1 handful coriander (cilantro) leaves
90 g (3¼ oz/1 cup) bean sprouts, washed
1 large red chilli, seeded and thinly sliced
1 teaspoon sesame oil
1 tablespoon Chinese rice wine

Cucumber and white fish stir-fry

»PREPARATION 30 MINUTES »COOKING TIME 25 MINUTES »SERVES 4–6

1 Combine the plain flour with the cornflour and five-spice in a shallow bowl and season. Dip the fish into the beaten egg white, drain off any excess, then toss gently in the flour mixture, shaking off any excess.

2 Fill a large saucepan one-third full of oil and heat to 180°C (350°F/ Gas 4), or until a cube of bread dropped into the oil browns in 15 seconds. Cook the fish pieces in batches, for 6 minutes, or until golden brown. Drain on crumpled paper towel.

3 Heat a wok over high heat, add the vegetable oil and swirl to coat. Add the onion wedges and stir-fry for 1 minute. Add the cucumber and stir-fry for 30 seconds.

4 Blend the extra cornflour with 2 tablespoons water and add to the wok along with the sesame oil, soy sauce, vinegar, sugar and fish sauce. Stir-fry for 3 minutes, or until the mixture boils and thickens. Add the fish and toss to coat in the sauce and heat through. Serve hot.

60 g (2¼ oz/½ cup) plain (all-purpose) flour

60 g (2¼ oz/½ cup) cornflour (cornstarch)

½ teaspoon Chinese five-spice

750 g (1 lb 10 oz) boneless, firm white fish fillets, cut into 3 cm (1¼ inch) cubes

2 egg whites, lightly beaten

oil, for deep-frying

1 tablespoon vegetable oil

1 onion, cut into wedges

1 telegraph (long) cucumber, halved, seeded and sliced diagonally

1 teaspoon cornflour (cornstarch), extra

¾ teaspoon sesame oil

1 tablespoon soy sauce

80 ml (2½ fl oz/⅓ cup) rice vinegar

1½ tablespoons soft brown sugar

3 teaspoons fish sauce

Noodles in black bean sauce

» PREPARATION 10 MINUTES
» COOKING TIME 10–15 MINUTES » SERVES 4

1 Cook 375 g (13 oz) of thin fresh egg noodles in a large pan of boiling water until just tender. Drain.

2 Rinse and chop 1 tablespoon dried, salted black beans. Thickly slice 3 spring onions (scallions).

3 Heat 1 teaspoon olive oil and 1 teaspoon sesame oil in a wok. Add 4 crushed garlic cloves and 1 tablespoon grated fresh ginger. Stir over low heat for 2 minutes. Add the black beans and stir for 2 minutes.

4 Add 125 ml (4 fl oz/½ cup) of vegetable stock, 1 tablespoon sugar, 2 tablespoons of hoisin sauce and 1 tablespoon black bean sauce to the wok and simmer for 5 minutes, or until the sauce is slightly reduced and thickened. Drain 235 g (8½ oz) tinned sliced bamboo shoots, and add them to the pan along with the noodles and spring onion. Stir until combined and heated through.

Egg fried rice

» PREPARATION 10 MINUTES
» COOKING TIME 10–15 MINUTES » SERVES 4

1 Chop 1 spring onion (scallion). Beat 4 eggs with 1 teaspoon of the spring onion and a pinch of salt. Cook 50 g (1 3/4 oz/⅓ cup) fresh or frozen peas in a saucepan of simmering water for 3–4 minutes for fresh or 1 minute for frozen.

2 Heat a wok over high heat, add 60 ml (2 fl oz/¼ cup) of oil and swirl to coat the base and side. Heat until very hot. Reduce the heat, add the egg and lightly scramble. Add 550 g (1 lb 4 oz/3 cups) cold cooked white long-grain rice before the egg is set too hard, increase the heat and stir to separate the rice grains and break the egg into small bits. Add the peas and the remaining spring onion and season with salt. Stir constantly for 1 minute.

Note You will need to cook 200 g (7 oz/1 cup) of rice for this recipe.

Tofu and vegetables

» PREPARATION 10 MINUTES
» COOKING TIME 10 MINUTES » SERVES 4–6

1 Heat 90 ml (3 fl oz) oil in a wok over medium heat. Break 125 g (4½ oz) rice vermicelli into short lengths. Cook in batches until crisp, then drain on paper towel.

2 Combine 1 tablespoon soy sauce, 1 tablespoon sherry, 1 tablespoon oyster sauce and 125 ml (4 fl oz/½ cup) vegetable stock.

3 Heat 1 tablespoon oil in the wok and cook 1 crushed garlic clove and 1 teaspoon grated fresh ginger over high heat for 1 minute. Add 375 g (13 oz) cubed firm tofu and cook for 3 minutes; remove. Cut 2 carrots into matchsticks and stir-fry with 250 g (9 oz) snow peas (mangetout) for 1 minute. Add the sauce mixture, cover and cook for 3 minutes. Return the tofu to the wok with 425 g (15 oz) tinned straw mushrooms, 4 thinly sliced spring onions (scallions) and 2 teaspoons cornflour combined with 2 teaspoons water. Stir until thickened. Serve with the vermicelli.

Pork noodle salad

»PREPARATION 20 MINUTES »COOKING TIME 35 MINUTES »SERVES 4–6

1 To make the broth, combine the chicken stock, coriander roots, makrut leaves, ginger and 250 ml (9 fl oz/1 cup) water in a saucepan. Simmer for 25 minutes, or until the liquid has reduced to 185 ml (6 fl oz/¾ cup). Strain and return to the pan.

2 Soak the vermicelli in boiling water for 6–7 minutes. Drain, then cut it into 3 cm (1¼ inch) lengths. Discard the woody stems from the wood ear fungus, then thinly slice. Combine the vermicelli, wood ear fungus, chilli, shallots, spring onion and garlic.

3 Bring the broth to the boil, add the pork and stir, breaking up any lumps, for 1–2 minutes, until the pork is cooked. Drain, then add to the vermicelli mixture.

4 In a separate bowl, combine the lime juice, fish sauce, palm sugar and white pepper, stirring until the sugar has dissolved. Add to the pork mixture along with the coriander and mix well. Season with salt.

5 To assemble, tear or shred the lettuce, then arrange on a serving dish. Spoon the pork and noodle mixture on the lettuce and garnish with the lime wedges, chilli and extra coriander.

Note Wood ear (also called black fungus) is a cultivated wood fungus. It is mainly available dried; it needs to be reconstituted in boiling water for a few minutes until it expands to five times its dried size before use.

Broth

250 ml (9 fl oz/1 cup) chicken stock
3 coriander (cilantro) roots
2 makrut (kaffir lime) leaves
3 cm (1¼ inch) piece fresh ginger, sliced

100 g (3½ oz) dried rice vermicelli
30 g (1 oz) wood ear fungus (see Note)
1 small red chilli, seeded and thinly sliced
2 red Asian shallots, thinly sliced
2 spring onions (scallions), thinly sliced
2 garlic cloves, crushed
250 g (9 oz) minced (ground) pork
60 ml (2 fl oz/¼ cup) lime juice
60 ml (2 fl oz/¼ cup) fish sauce
1½ tablespoons grated palm sugar (jaggery)
¼ teaspoon ground white pepper
1 large handful coriander (cilantro) leaves, chopped
oakleaf or coral lettuce, to serve
lime wedges, to garnish
chilli strips, to garnish
coriander (cilantro) leaves, extra, to garnish

Oriental mushrooms with hokkien noodles

»PREPARATION 35 MINUTES »COOKING TIME 10 MINUTES »SERVES 4

1 Soak the hokkien noodles in boiling water for 2 minutes. Drain and set them aside.

2 Cut the red capsicum in half, remove the seeds and membrane and slice. Slice the spring onions and shiitake mushrooms.

3 Heat the sesame and peanut oils in a wok and swirl to coat the base and side. Add the garlic, ginger and spring onion. Stir-fry over high heat for 2 minutes. Add the capsicum and the oyster and shiitake mushrooms.

Stir-fry the vegetables over high heat for 3 minutes, until the mushrooms are golden brown.

4 Stir in the noodles, then add the chives, cashews, kecap manis and soy sauce and stir-fry for 3 minutes, or until the noodles are coated in the sauce.

Note Kecap manis is an Indonesian sweet soy sauce. If you are unable to find it, use soy sauce sweetened with a little soft brown sugar.

250 g (9 oz) hokkien (egg) noodles
1 red capsicum (pepper)
6 spring onions (scallions)
200 g (7 oz) shiitake mushrooms
1 teaspoon sesame oil
1 tablespoon peanut oil
2 garlic cloves, crushed
2 tablespoons grated fresh ginger
200 g (7 oz) oyster mushrooms
125 g (4½ oz) snipped garlic chives
40 g (1½ oz/¼ cup) cashew nuts
2 tablespoons kecap manis (see Note)
60 ml (2 fl oz/¼ cup) salt-reduced
  soy sauce

Yoghurt rice

» PREPARATION 10 MINUTES + 3 HOURS SOAKING » COOKING TIME 15 MINUTES » SERVES 4

1 Soak the dals in the boiling water for 3 hours. Wash the rice under cold running water until the water runs clear. Drain.

2 Put the rice and 500 ml (17 fl oz/ 2 cups) water in a saucepan and bring rapidly to the boil. Stir, cover, reduce the heat to a slow simmer and cook for 10 minutes. Leave for 15 minutes before fluffing up the rice with a fork.

3 Drain the dals and pat dry with paper towel. For the final seasoning, heat the oil in a small saucepan over low heat. Add the mustard seeds, then cover and shake the pan until the seeds start to pop. Add the curry leaves, dried chillies and drained dals and fry for 2 minutes, stirring occasionally. Stir in the turmeric and asafoetida.

4 Put the yoghurt in a large bowl, pour the fried dal mixture into the yoghurt and mix thoroughly. Mix the rice into the spicy yoghurt, then season with salt to taste. Serve cold, but before serving, stand the rice at room temperature for 10 minutes.

Notes In India, dal relates to any type of dried split pea, bean or lentil. This is a popular dish for taking on journeys as the dish is served cold and the acid in the yoghurt acts as a preservative.

Available as a yellowish powder or resin, asafoetida is made from the dried resin of a type of fennel. It is used as a flavour enhancer in Indian and Middle Eastern cooking.

2 tablespoons urad dal (see Notes)
2 tablespoons chana dal (see Notes)
250 ml (9 fl oz/1 cup) boiling water
225 g (8 oz) basmati rice
2 tablespoons oil
1/2 teaspoon mustard seeds
12 curry leaves
3 dried chillies
1/4 teaspoon ground turmeric
pinch asafoetida (see Notes)
500 g (1 lb 2 oz/2 cups) thick plain yoghurt

55 Balinese seafood curry

50 Chicken laksa

60 Panang beef

62 Malaysian fish head curry

64 Yellow vegetable curry

Curry meals

Chicken laksa

1 Toast the coriander and cumin seeds in a frying pan over medium heat for 1–2 minutes, until fragrant, tossing constantly to prevent them from burning. Grind finely using a mortar and pestle or a spice grinder.

2 Put all the spices, onion, ginger, garlic, lemon grass, macadamia nuts, chillies and shrimp paste in a food processor or blender. Add 125 ml (4 fl oz/½ cup) of the stock and blend to a paste.

3 Heat the oil in a wok or large saucepan over low heat. Gently cook the paste for 3–5 minutes, stirring constantly to prevent it burning or sticking to the bottom of the pan. Add the remaining stock and bring to the boil over high heat. Reduce the heat to medium and simmer for 15 minutes, or until reduced slightly. Add the chicken pieces

and simmer for 4–5 minutes. Add the coconut milk, lime leaves, lime juice, fish sauce and sugar. Simmer for 5 minutes over medium–low heat. Do not bring to the boil or cover with a lid, as the coconut milk will split.

4 Meanwhile, put the vermicelli in a heatproof bowl, cover with boiling water and soak for 6–7 minutes, or until softened. Drain and divide among large serving bowls with the bean sprouts. Ladle the soup over the top and garnish with some tofu strips, mint and coriander leaves. Serve with a wedge of lime.

Note To roast the shrimp paste, wrap the paste in foil and put under a hot grill (broiler) for 1 minute.

1½ tablespoons coriander seeds
1 tablespoon cumin seeds
1 teaspoon ground turmeric
1 onion, roughly chopped
1 tablespoon roughly chopped ginger
3 garlic cloves
3 lemon grass stems, white part only, sliced
6 macadamia nuts
4–6 small red chillies
3 teaspoons shrimp paste, roasted (see Note)
1 litre (35 fl oz/4 cups) chicken stock
60 ml (2 fl oz/¼ cup) oil
400 g (14 oz) chicken thigh fillets, cut into 2 cm (¾ inch) pieces
750 ml (26 fl oz/3 cups) coconut milk
4 makrut (kaffir lime) leaves
2½ tablespoons lime juice
2 tablespoons fish sauce
2 tablespoons grated palm sugar (jaggery) or soft brown sugar
250 g (9 oz) dried rice vermicelli
90 g (3¼ oz/1 cup) bean sprouts, trimmed
4 fried tofu puffs, cut into thin batons
3 tablespoons chopped Vietnamese mint
1 handful coriander (cilantro) leaves
lime wedges, to serve

Sri Lankan fish fillets in tomato curry

»PREPARATION 20 MINUTES »COOKING TIME 20 MINUTES »SERVES 6

1 To make the marinade, put the lemon juice, coconut vinegar, cumin seeds, ground turmeric, cayenne pepper and 1 teaspoon salt in a shallow, non-metallic container and mix together thoroughly.

2 Carefully remove any remaining bones from the fish with tweezers and cut the flesh into 2.5 x 10 cm (1 x 4 inch) pieces. Add the fish to the marinade and gently toss until well coated. Cover with plastic wrap and refrigerate for 30 minutes.

3 Heat a non-stick wok over high heat, add the oil and swirl to coat the base and side. Reduce the heat to low and add the onion, garlic, ginger and mustard seeds. Cook, stirring frequently, for 5 minutes. Add the fish and marinade, diced tomatoes, coriander, chilli and palm sugar to the wok and cover. Simmer gently, stirring occasionally, for 10–15 minutes, or until the fish is cooked and just flakes when tested with the tines of a fork. Serve with steamed rice.

Note Coconut vinegar is made from the sap of various palm trees.

60 ml (2 fl oz/¼ cup) lemon juice
60 ml (2 fl oz/¼ cup) coconut vinegar (see Note)
2 teaspoons cumin seeds
1 teaspoon ground turmeric
1 teaspoon cayenne pepper
1 kg (2 lb 4 oz) skinless, boneless firm white fish fillets
60 ml (2 fl oz/¼ cup) oil
1 large onion, finely chopped
3 large garlic cloves, crushed
2 tablespoons grated fresh ginger
1 teaspoon black mustard seeds
1.2 kg (2 lb 12 oz) tinned diced tomatoes
3 tablespoons finely chopped coriander (cilantro)
2 small green chillies, seeded and finely chopped
2 tablespoons grated palm sugar (jaggery)
steamed rice, to serve

Thai musaman beef curry

»PREPARATION 30 MINUTES »COOKING TIME 2 HOURS »SERVES 4

1 Put the tamarind pulp in a heatproof bowl, add the boiling water and set aside to cool. Mash the pulp with your fingertips to dissolve it, then strain and reserve the liquid, and discard the pulp.

2 Heat a non-stick wok over high heat, add the oil and swirl to coat the base and side. Add the beef in batches and cook over high heat for 5 minutes, or until browned all over. Reduce the heat, add the coconut milk and cardamom pods. Simmer for 1 hour, until the beef is tender.

Remove the beef from the wok. Strain the cooking liquid into a bowl and reserve.

3 Heat the coconut cream in the cleaned wok and stir in the curry paste. Cook for 10 minutes, or until the oil starts to separate from the cream. Add the fish sauce, onions, potatoes, beef mixture, palm sugar, peanuts, tamarind water and the reserved cooking liquid. Simmer for about 30 minutes, or until the sauce has thickened and the meat is tender.

1 tablespoon tamarind pulp

125 ml (4 fl oz/½ cup) boiling water

2 tablespoons oil

750 g (1 lb 10 oz) lean stewing beef, cubed

500 ml (17 fl oz/2 cups) coconut milk

4 cardamom pods, bruised

500 ml (17 fl oz/2 cups) coconut cream

2 tablespoons ready-made Musaman curry paste

2 tablespoons fish sauce

8 pickling onions

8 baby potatoes

2 tablespoons grated palm sugar (jaggery)

80 g (2¾ oz/½ cup) unsalted peanuts, roasted and ground

Butter chicken

»PREPARATION 10 MINUTES »COOKING TIME 35 MINUTES »SERVES 4–6

1 Heat a wok until very hot, add 1 tablespoon oil and swirl to coat the base and side. Add half the chicken and stir-fry for 4 minutes, or until nicely browned. Remove from the wok. Add a little extra oil, if needed, and brown the remaining chicken. Remove from the wok and set aside.

2 Reduce the heat to medium, add the butter or ghee to the wok and stir until melted. Add the garam masala, paprika, coriander, ginger, chilli powder, cinnamon stick and cardamom pods, and stir-fry for 1 minute, or until the spices are fragrant. Return all of the chicken to the wok and mix until coated in the spices. Add the tomato passata and sugar and simmer, stirring, for 15 minutes, or until the chicken is tender and the sauce is thick. Stir in the yoghurt, cream and lemon juice and simmer for 5 minutes, or until the sauce has thickened slightly. Serve with poppadoms.

2 tablespoons peanut oil
1 kg (2 lb 4 oz) boneless, skinless chicken thighs, quartered
60 g (2¼ oz) butter or ghee
2 teaspoons garam masala
2 teaspoons sweet paprika
2 teaspoons ground coriander
1 tablespoon finely chopped fresh ginger
¼ teaspoon chilli powder
1 cinnamon stick
6 cardamom pods, bruised
350 g (12 oz) tomato passata (puréed tomatoes)
1 tablespoon sugar
60 g (2¼ oz/¼ cup) plain yoghurt
125 ml (4 fl oz/½ cup) pouring cream
1 tablespoon lemon juice
poppadoms, to serve

Thai duck and pineapple curry

» PREPARATION 10 MINUTES
» COOKING TIME 15 MINUTES » SERVES 4–6

1 Slice 8 spring onions (scallions) on the diagonal into short lengths. Chop a 750 g (1 lb 10 oz) Chinese roast duck. Drain 450 g (1 lb) of tinned pineapple pieces in syrup.

2 Heat a wok until very hot, add 1 tablespoon peanut oil and swirl to coat. Stir-fry the spring onion, 2–4 tablespoons Thai red curry paste and 2 crushed garlic cloves for 1 minute, or until fragrant.

3 Add the duck, pineapple, 400 ml (14 fl oz) coconut milk, 3 makrut (kaffir lime) leaves, 1½ tablespoons chopped coriander (cilantro) leaves and 1 tablespoon chopped mint. Bring to the boil, then reduce the heat and simmer for 10 minutes, or until the duck is heated through and the sauce has thickened slightly. Stir in another 1½ tablespoons chopped coriander (cilantro) leaves and 1 tablespoon chopped mint. Serve with jasmine rice.

Thai coconut vegetables

» PREPARATION 15–20 MINUTES
» COOKING TIME 15 MINUTES » SERVES 4–6

1 Cut 2 small onions into wedges. Heat 1 tablespoon oil in a wok and stir-fry the onion and 1 teaspoon ground cumin over medium heat for 2 minutes, or until the onion is golden. Add 150 g (5½ oz) of cauliflower florets and stir-fry over high heat for 2 minutes. Stir in 1 chopped red capsicum (pepper), 2 sliced celery stalks and 185 g (6½ oz/1½ cups) grated pumpkin (winter squash). Stir-fry over high heat for 2 minutes, or until the vegetables have begun to soften.

2 Add 250 ml (9 fl oz/1 cup) of coconut milk, 250 ml (9 fl oz/1 cup) vegetable stock and 1 tablespoon sweet chilli sauce and bring to the boil. Reduce the heat and cook for 8 minutes, until the vegetables are almost tender. Add 1 tablespoon finely chopped coriander (cilantro) and 150 g (5½ oz) halved green beans. Cook for 2 minutes, or until the beans are just tender. Serve with steamed rice.

Madras beef curry

» PREPARATION 20 MINUTES
» COOKING TIME 1 HOURS 30 MINUTES » SERVES 6

1 Trim the fat and sinew from 1 kg (2 lb 4 oz) skirt or chuck steak, and cut it into 2.5 cm (1 inch) cubes.

2 Combine 1 tablespoon ground coriander, 1½ tablespoons ground cumin, 1 teaspoon brown mustard seeds, ½ teaspoon cracked black pepper, 1 teaspoon chilli powder and 1 teaspoon ground turmeric in a small bowl. Add 2 teaspoons crushed garlic, 2 teaspoons grated fresh ginger, 1 teaspoon salt and 2–3 tablespoons white vinegar. Mix to a smooth paste.

3 Heat 1 tablespoon oil in a large frying pan. Cook 1 chopped onion over medium heat until just soft. Add the spice paste and stir for 1 minute, then stir in the meat until coated. Add 250 ml (9 fl oz/ 1 cup) beef stock and 60 g (2¼ oz/ ¼ cup) tomato paste (concentrated purée), then simmer, covered, for 1½ hours, until the meat is tender. Serve with steamed rice.

Balinese seafood curry

»PREPARATION 20 MINUTES »COOKING TIME 20 MINUTES »SERVES 6

1 To make the curry paste, score a cross in the base of each tomato. Put in a heatproof bowl and cover with boiling water. Leave for 30 seconds, then transfer to cold water, drain and peel away the skin from the cross. Cut the tomatoes in half, scoop out the seeds and chop the flesh. Put in a food processor with the remaining paste ingredients and blend until a thick paste forms.

2 Peel the prawns and gently pull out the dark vein from each prawn back, starting at the head end.

3 Pour the lime juice into a bowl and season. Add the swordfish, coat well and marinate for 20 minutes.

4 Heat a non-stick wok over high heat, add the oil and swirl to coat the base and side. Add the onion, chilli and curry paste, and cook, stirring occasionally, over low heat for 10 minutes, or until fragrant. Add the swordfish and prawns, and stir to coat in the curry paste mixture. Cook for 3 minutes, until the prawns just turn pink, then add the calamari and cook for a further 1 minute. Add the stock and bring to the boil, then reduce the heat and simmer for 2 minutes, or until the seafood is cooked and tender. Season to taste and garnish with the shredded basil.

Notes If you can't find shrimp powder, put some dried shrimp in a mortar and pestle or small food processor and grind or process into a fine powder.
Use a non-stick or stainless steel wok to cook this recipe as the tamarind will react with the metal in a regular wok and badly taint the dish.

Curry paste
2 tomatoes
5 small red chillies, seeded and chopped
5 garlic cloves, chopped
2 lemon grass stems, white part only, sliced
1 tablespoon coriander seeds, dry-roasted and ground
1 teaspoon shrimp powder, dry-roasted (see Notes)
1 tablespoon ground almonds
¼ teaspoon ground nutmeg
1 teaspoon ground turmeric
3 tablespoons tamarind purée

400 g (14 oz) raw prawns (shrimp)
1 tablespoon lime juice
250 g (9 oz) swordfish, cut into 3 cm (1¼ inch) cubes
60 ml (2 fl oz/¼ cup) oil
2 red onions, chopped
2 small red chillies, seeded and sliced
250 g (9 oz) calamari tubes, cut into 1 cm (½ inch) rings
125 ml (4 fl oz/½ cup) fish stock
shredded Thai basil, to garnish

Lamb kofta

»PREPARATION 25 MINUTES   »COOKING TIME 50 MINUTES   »SERVES 4–6

1 Line a baking tray with baking paper. Place the minced lamb in a large bowl. Add the onion, chilli, ginger, garlic, cardamom, egg and breadcrumbs, and season well. Mix until combined. Roll tablespoons of the mixture into balls, and place them on the prepared tray.

2 Heat the ghee in a frying pan and cook the meatballs in two batches over medium heat for 5 minutes at a time, or until browned all over. Transfer all of the meatballs to a large bowl.

3 To make the sauce, heat the ghee in the cleaned pan, add the onion, chilli, ginger, garlic and turmeric, and cook, stirring, over low heat until the onion is soft. Add the coriander, cumin, chilli, vinegar, 350 ml (12 fl oz/1⅓ cups) water and the meatballs, and stir gently. Cover and simmer for 30 minutes.

4 Stir in the combined yoghurt and coconut milk. Simmer for a further 10 minutes with the pan partially covered. Serve with steamed rice.

1 kg (2 lb 4 oz) minced (ground) lamb
1 onion, finely chopped
2 green chillies, finely chopped
3 teaspoons grated fresh ginger
3 garlic cloves, crushed
1 teaspoon ground cardamom
1 egg
25 g (1 oz/⅓ cup) fresh breadcrumbs
2 tablespoons ghee or oil

Sauce
1 tablespoon ghee or oil
1 onion, sliced
1 green chilli, finely chopped
3 teaspoons grated fresh ginger
2 garlic cloves, crushed
1 teaspoon ground turmeric
3 teaspoons ground coriander
2 teaspoons ground cumin
1 teaspoon chilli powder
2 tablespoons white vinegar
185 g (6½ oz/¾ cup) plain yoghurt
310 ml (10¾ fl oz/1¼ cups) coconut milk
steamed rice, to serve

Chicken kapitan

»PREPARATION 35 MINUTES »COOKING TIME 30 MINUTES »SERVES 4–6

1 Put the shrimp in a frying pan and dry-fry over low heat, shaking the pan regularly, for 3 minutes, or until the shrimp are dark orange and are giving off a strong aroma. Transfer the shrimp to a mortar and pestle and pound until finely ground. Set aside.

2 Put half the oil with the chilli, garlic, lemon grass, turmeric and candlenuts in a food processor and process in short bursts until very finely chopped, regularly scraping down the side of the bowl with a rubber spatula.

3 Heat the remaining oil in a wok or frying pan, add the onion and ¼ teaspoon salt and cook over low heat for 8 minutes, or until golden, stirring regularly. Take care not to let the onion burn. Add the spice

mixture and nearly all the ground shrimp meat, setting a little aside to use as garnish. Stir for 5 minutes. If the mixture sticks to the bottom of the pan, add 2 tablespoons of the coconut milk to the mixture. It is important to cook the mixture thoroughly to develop the flavours.

4 Add the chicken to the wok and stir well. Cook for 5 minutes, or until the chicken begins to brown. Stir in the remaining coconut milk and 250 ml (9 fl oz/1 cup) water. Bring to the boil, then reduce the heat and simmer for 7 minutes, or until the chicken is cooked and the sauce is thick. Add the coconut cream and bring the mixture back to the boil, stirring constantly. Add the lime juice and serve immediately, sprinkled with the reserved ground shrimp. Serve with steamed rice.

30 g (1 oz) small dried shrimp
80 ml (2½ fl oz/⅓ cup) oil
4–8 red chillies, seeded and finely chopped
4 garlic cloves, finely chopped
3 lemon grass stems (white part only), finely chopped
2 teaspoons ground turmeric
10 candlenuts
2 large onions, chopped
500 g (1 lb 2 oz) boneless, skinless chicken thighs, chopped
250 ml (9 fl oz/1 cup) coconut milk
125 ml (4 fl oz/½ cup) coconut cream
2 tablespoons lime juice
steamed rice, to serve

Nasi lemak

» PREPARATION 40 MINUTES   » COOKING TIME 2 HOURS 40 MINUTES   » SERVES 4

1 To make the rendang, put the onion, garlic and 1 tablespoon of water into a food processor and blend to form a smooth paste.

2 Pour the coconut milk into a wok and bring to the boil. Reduce the heat to medium and cook, stirring occasionally, for 15 minutes, or until the milk is reduced by half and the oil has separated, but do not allow the milk to brown. Add the cumin, coriander, fennel and cloves to the wok and stir for 1 minute. Stir in the meat and cook for 2 minutes, or until it browns.

3 Add the chilli, lemon juice, lemon grass, sugar and prepared rendang mixture. Cover and cook over medium heat, stirring often, for about 2 hours, or until the liquid is reduced and thickened. Remove the cover and continue cooking until the oil separates again. Take care not to burn the sauce. The curry is cooked when it is brown and dry.

4 Meanwhile, to make the coconut rice, put the rice, shallots, ginger, fenugreek, pandanus leaves and 1 teaspoon salt in a saucepan. Pour enough coconut milk over the rice so there is 2 cm (¾ inch) of liquid above the surface of the rice. Cover and cook until dry, then remove the pandanus leaf, sprinkle the rest of the coconut milk over the rice, then fluff up the grains. Leave the rice for 15 minutes, until the coconut milk is completely absorbed.

5 To make the sambal, heat the oil in a wok, add the shallots, garlic, lemon grass, shrimp paste and chilli paste, and stir-fry until fragrant. Add the ikan bilis and stir-fry for a few more minutes. Mix in the sugar and the lime juice. Serve with the rendang and rice.

Note Ikan bilis are dried anchovies. In Malaysia, nasi lemak is served for breakfast.

Rendang
2 onions, roughly chopped
2 garlic cloves, crushed
400 ml (14 fl oz) tinned coconut milk
2 teaspoons ground cumin
2 teaspoons ground coriander
½ teaspoon ground fennel
¼ teaspoon ground cloves
1.5 kg (3 lb 5 oz) chuck steak, cut into cubes
4–6 small red chillies, chopped
1 tablespoon lemon juice
1 lemon grass stem, white part only, bruised and cut lengthways
2 teaspoons grated palm sugar (jaggery)

Coconut rice
300 g (10½ oz/1½ cups) long-grain rice
2 red Asian shallots
2 slices ginger
pinch fenugreek seeds
2 pandanus leaves, knotted
400 ml (14 fl oz) tinned coconut milk

Sambal ikan bilis
60 ml (2 fl oz/¼ cup) oil
5 red Asian shallots, sliced
2 garlic cloves, crushed
1 lemon grass stem, white part only, thinly sliced
½ teaspoon shrimp paste
2 tablespoons chilli paste
100 g (3½ oz) ikan bilis, soaked and washed (see Note)
1 teaspoon sugar
2 tablespoons lime juice

Panang beef

1 To make the curry paste, put the chillies in a bowl and cover with boiling water. Soak for 20 minutes, or until softened. Remove the seeds and roughly chop the flesh. Put the chopped chillies in a food processor along with the red shallots, garlic, ground coriander, ground cumin, white pepper, lemon grass, galangal, coriander roots, shrimp paste and roasted peanuts and process until a smooth paste forms. You might need to add a little water if the paste is too thick.

2 Scoop off the really thick cream from the top of the tin of coconut cream and put this thick cream in a wok. Cook over medium heat for 10 minutes, or until the oil starts to separate from the cream. Stir in 8 tablespoons of the curry paste. Cook for 5–8 minutes, stirring often, until fragrant. Add the beef, coconut milk, peanut butter, makrut leaves and the remaining coconut cream and cook for 8 minutes, or until the beef just starts to change colour. Reduce the heat to low and simmer for 30 minutes, or until the beef is tender, stirring every few minutes to prevent it from catching on the bottom.

3 Stir in the lime juice, fish sauce and sugar. Serve the beef with some steamed rice and garnish with the roasted peanuts and basil.

Curry paste

- 8–10 large dried red chillies
- 6 red Asian shallots, chopped
- 6 garlic cloves, chopped
- 1 teaspoon ground coriander
- 1 tablespoon ground cumin
- 1 teaspoon white pepper
- 2 lemon grass stems, white part only, bruised, sliced
- 1 tablespoon chopped fresh galangal
- 6 coriander (cilantro) roots
- 2 teaspoons shrimp paste
- 2 tablespoons roasted peanuts

- 400 ml (14 fl oz) tinned coconut cream (do not shake)
- 1 kg (2 lb 4 oz) round or blade steak, cut into 1 cm (½ inch) slices
- 400 ml (14 fl oz) tinned coconut milk
- 90 g (3¼ oz/⅓ cup) crunchy peanut butter
- 4 makrut (kaffir lime) leaves
- 60 ml (2 fl oz/¼ cup) lime juice
- 2½ tablespoons fish sauce
- 3–4 tablespoons grated palm sugar (jaggery)
- steamed rice, to serve
- chopped roasted peanuts, to garnish
- Thai basil, to garnish

Mild Vietnamese chicken curry

»PREPARATION 30 MINUTES + MARINATING »COOKING TIME 1 HOUR 10 MINUTES »SERVES 6

1 Pat the chicken pieces dry with paper towel. Put the curry powder, sugar, ½ teaspoon black pepper and 2 teaspoons salt in a bowl, and mix together well. Rub the mixture onto the chicken, then place the chicken on a plate, cover with plastic wrap and refrigerate overnight.

2 Break the rice vermicelli into short lengths. Heat 90 ml (3 fl oz) of the oil in a wok over medium heat. Cook the vermicelli in batches until crisp, adding more oil when necessary. Drain on paper towel and set aside.

3 Reheat the wok over high heat, add 80 ml (2½ fl oz/⅓ cup) of the oil and swirl to coat the base and side. Add the sweet potato and cook over medium heat for 3 minutes, or until lightly golden. Remove with a slotted spoon and set aside.

4 Remove all but 2 tablespoons of oil from the wok. Stir-fry the onion for 5 minutes. Add the garlic, lemon grass and bay leaves, and cook for 2 minutes. Add the chicken pieces and cook, stirring, over medium heat for 5 minutes, or until well coated in the mixture and starting to change colour.

5 Add 250 ml (9 fl oz/1 cup) water and simmer, covered, over low heat for 20 minutes, stirring occasionally. Add the carrot, sweet potato and coconut milk. Simmer, uncovered, stirring occasionally, for 30 minutes, or until the chicken is cooked and tender. Be careful not to break up the sweet potato cubes. Serve with the crisp vermicelli.

4 large chicken quarters (leg and thigh), skin and excess fat removed, cut into thirds
1 tablespoon curry powder
1 teaspoon caster (superfine) sugar
125 g (4½ oz) dried rice vermicelli
250 ml (9 fl oz/1 cup) oil
500 g (1 lb 2 oz) orange sweet potato, peeled, cut into 3 cm (1¼ inch) cubes
1 large onion, cut into thin wedges
4 garlic cloves, chopped
1 lemon grass stem, white part only, finely chopped
2 bay leaves
1 large carrot, cut diagonally into 1 cm (½ inch) pieces
400 ml (14 fl oz) coconut milk

Malaysian fish head curry

1 To make the curry paste, put all the ingredients in a food processor or blender and blend to a smooth paste, adding a little water if needed.

2 Lift the thick cream off the top of the coconut cream. Put the cream in a non-stick wok and bring to the boil. Simmer for 10 minutes, until the oil starts to separate from the cream. Add the curry paste and cook for 5 minutes, until fragrant. Add the curry leaves, curry powder and turmeric and cook for 1 minute.

3 Stir in the stock, tamarind purée, fish sauce, sugar and the remaining coconut cream and bring to the boil for 1 minute. Add the eggplant and okra, reduce the heat and simmer for 15 minutes. Add the fish heads and cook for a further 5 minutes, turning to cook evenly. Stir in the tomato and green chilli until heated through; the vegetables should be tender and the fish eyes opaque. Season to taste and serve with steamed rice.

Curry paste
4 garlic cloves, chopped
4 red Asian shallots, chopped
1 lemon grass stem, white part only, finely chopped
3 cm (1¼ inch) piece fresh galangal, finely chopped
2 large red chillies, chopped

400 ml (14 fl oz) tinned coconut cream (do not shake)
10 curry leaves
2 tablespoons Malaysian seafood curry powder
½ teaspoon ground turmeric

500 ml (17 fl oz/2 cups) fish stock
2 tablespoons tamarind purée
2 tablespoons fish sauce
1 tablespoon sugar
200 g (7 oz) eggplant (aubergine), cut into 1 cm (½ inch) slices
150 g (5½ oz) okra, cut into 1 cm (½ inch) slices
4 x 200 g (7 oz) fish heads (ask your fishmonger to clean and scale them)
2 ripe tomatoes, cut into eighths
2 large green chillies, cut into 1 cm (½ inch) slices
steamed rice, to serve

Prawn laksa

»PREPARATION 30 MINUTES »COOKING TIME 35 MINUTES »SERVES 4–6

1 Peel the prawns, leaving the tails intact. Gently pull out the dark vein from each prawn back, starting at the head end.

2 Dry-fry the coriander seeds in a small frying pan over medium heat for 1–2 minutes, or until fragrant, tossing constantly. Finely grind using a mortar and pestle or spice grinder. Repeat the process with the cumin seeds.

3 Put the ground coriander and cumin, turmeric, onion, ginger, garlic, lemon grass, candlenuts, chilli and shrimp paste in a food processor or blender. Add about 125 ml (4 fl oz/½ cup) of the stock and blend to a fine paste.

4 Heat a wok over low heat, add the oil and swirl to coat. Cook the paste for 3–5 minutes, stirring constantly. Pour in the remaining stock and bring to the boil, then reduce the heat and simmer for 15 minutes, or until reduced slightly. Add the coconut milk, makrut leaves, lime juice, fish sauce and sugar. Simmer for 5 minutes. Add the prawns and simmer for 2 minutes, or until pink and cooked. Do not boil or cover.

5 Meanwhile, soak the vermicelli in boiling water for 6–7 minutes, until soft. Drain and divide among serving bowls along with most of the bean sprouts. Ladle on the hot soup then top with the tofu, mint, coriander and the remaining bean sprouts. Serve with lime wedges.

750 g (1 lb 10 oz) raw prawns (shrimp)
1½ tablespoons coriander seeds
1 tablespoon cumin seeds
1 teaspoon ground turmeric
1 onion, roughly chopped
2 teaspoons roughly chopped fresh ginger
3 garlic cloves
3 lemon grass stems, white part only, sliced
6 candlenuts or macadamia nuts, roughly chopped
4–6 small red chillies, roughly chopped
2–3 teaspoons shrimp paste
1 litre (35 fl oz/4 cups) chicken stock
60 ml (2 fl oz/¼ cup) vegetable oil
750 ml (26 fl oz/3 cups) coconut milk
4 fresh makrut (kaffir lime) leaves
2½ tablespoons lime juice
2 tablespoons fish sauce
2 tablespoons grated palm sugar (jaggery) or soft brown sugar
250 g (8 oz) dried rice vermicelli
90 g (3¼ oz/1 cup) bean sprouts, trimmed
4 fried tofu puffs, cut into thin strips
3 tablespoons chopped Vietnamese mint
1 small handful coriander (cilantro) leaves
lime wedges, to serve

Yellow vegetable curry

»PREPARATION 20 MINUTES »COOKING TIME 20 MINUTES »SERVES 4

1 To make the curry paste, soak the chillies in boiling water for about 20 minutes. Drain and chop. Heat a frying pan, add the peppercorns, coriander seeds, cumin seeds and turmeric and dry-fry over medium heat for 3 minutes. Transfer to a mortar and pestle or food processor and finely grind. Put the ground spices, chilli, galangal, garlic, ginger, shallots, lemon grass and shrimp paste in a mortar and pestle and pound until smooth. Stir in the lime zest.

2 Heat a wok over medium heat, add the oil and swirl to coat the base and side. Add 2 tablespoons of the curry paste and cook for 1 minute. Add 250 ml (9 fl oz/1 cup) of the coconut cream. Bring to the boil, then simmer for 10 minutes, or until the liquid becomes thick and the oil starts to separate from the cream. Add the vegetable stock, vegetables and remaining coconut cream and cook for 5 minutes, or until the vegetables are tender. Stir in the fish sauce and sugar. Garnish with chilli and coriander.

Yellow curry paste

8 small dried red chillies
1 teaspoon black peppercorns
2 teaspoons coriander seeds
2 teaspoons cumin seeds
1 teaspoon ground turmeric
1½ tablespoons chopped fresh galangal
5 garlic cloves, chopped
1 teaspoon grated fresh ginger
5 red Asian shallots, chopped
2 lemon grass stems, white part only, chopped
1 teaspoon shrimp paste
1 teaspoon finely chopped lime zest

2 tablespoons peanut oil
500 ml (17 fl oz/2 cups) coconut cream
125 ml (4 fl oz/½ cup) vegetable stock
150 g (5½ oz) snake (yard-long) beans, cut into 3 cm (1¼ inch) lengths
150 g (5½ oz) baby corn
1 slender eggplant (aubergine), cut into 1 cm (½ inch) slices
100 g (3½ oz) cauliflower, cut into small florets
2 small zucchini (courgettes), cut into 1 cm (½ inch) slices
1 small red capsicum (pepper), seeded, membrane removed and cut into 1 cm (½ inch) slices
1½ tablespoons fish sauce
1 teaspoon grated palm sugar (jaggery)
chopped red chilli, to garnish
coriander (cilantro) leaves, to garnish

Balti lamb

» PREPARATION 15 MINUTES » COOKING TIME 1 HOUR 25 MINUTES » SERVES 4

1 Put the cubed lamb, 1 tablespoon of the curry paste and the boiling water in a wok and mix together. Bring to the boil over high heat, then reduce the heat to very low. Cook, covered, for 40–50 minutes, or until the meat is almost cooked through. Drain, set the meat aside, and reserve the sauce.

2 Heat the ghee in a clean wok over medium heat. Add the onion and cook for 5–7 minutes, or until soft. Add the garlic and garam masala and cook for a further 2–3 minutes. Increase the heat, add the remaining curry paste and return the lamb to the wok. Cook for 5 minutes, or until the meat has browned. Slowly add the reserved sauce and simmer over low heat, stirring occasionally, for 15 minutes. Add the chopped coriander and 250 ml (9 fl oz/1 cup) water and simmer for 15 minutes, or until the meat is tender and the sauce has thickened slightly. Season to taste.

3 Garnish with the extra coriander leaves and serve with poppadoms and steamed rice.

1 kg (2 lb 4 oz) lamb leg steaks, cut into 3 cm (1 ¼ inch) cubes
5 tablespoons ready-made Balti curry paste
1 litre (35 fl oz/4 cups) boiling water
2 tablespoons ghee or vegetable oil
1 large onion, finely chopped
3 garlic cloves, crushed
1 tablespoon garam masala
2 tablespoons chopped coriander (cilantro) leaves, plus extra, to garnish
poppadoms, to serve
steamed rice, to serve

71 North Vietnamese braised pork leg

68 Thai rice noodle soup with duck

76 Fish ball and noodle soup

77 Thai sweet and sour chicken soup

78 Pork and corn ramen noodle soup

Soups,
stews and hotpots

Thai rice noodle soup with duck

» PREPARATION 40 MINUTES » COOKING TIME 25 MINUTES » SERVES 4–6

1 Cut off and discard the duck's head. Remove the skin and fat from the duck, leaving the neck intact. Carefully remove the flesh from the bones and set aside. Cut any visible fat from the carcass along with the parson's nose, then discard. Break the carcass into large pieces and put them in a large stockpot with 2 litres (70 fl oz/8 cups) water.

2 Bruise the coriander roots and stems with the back of a knife. Add to the stockpot with the galangal and bring to the boil. Skim off any scum from the surface. Boil over medium heat for 10 minutes. Strain the stock through a fine sieve, then discard the carcass and return the stock to a large clean wok.

3 Slice the duck flesh into strips and add to the stock with the spring onion, Chinese broccoli, garlic, fish sauce, hoisin sauce, sugar and white pepper. Gently bring to the boil.

4 Put the noodles in a heatproof bowl, cover with boiling water and then gently separate them. Drain well and refresh under cold water. Divide the noodles evenly among serving bowls and pour over the soup. If desired, garnish with the fried garlic and coriander leaves. Serve immediately.

Note Chinese roast duck is available from Chinese barbecue shops.

1 whole Chinese roast duck (see Note)
4 coriander (cilantro) roots and stems, well rinsed
50 g (1¾ oz) galangal, sliced
4 spring onions (scallions), sliced
400 g (14 oz) Chinese broccoli (gai larn), cut into 5 cm (2 inch) lengths
2 garlic cloves, crushed
60 ml (2 fl oz/¼ cup) fish sauce
1 tablespoon hoisin sauce
2 teaspoons grated palm sugar (jaggery) or soft brown sugar
½ teaspoon ground white pepper
500 g (1 lb 2 oz) fresh rice noodles
crisp fried garlic, to garnish (optional)
coriander (cilantro) leaves, to garnish (optional)

Thai pumpkin and coconut soup

»PREPARATION 20 MINUTES »COOKING TIME 30 MINUTES »SERVES 4

1 Peel the prawns and gently pull out the dark vein from each prawn back, starting from the head end.

2 Wrap the shrimp paste in foil and place under a hot grill (broiler) for 1 minute. Unwrap the foil and put the shrimp paste in a food processor with the chilli, peppercorns, chilli paste, garlic and a pinch of salt, and process until smooth. Set aside.

3 Heat a wok over high heat, add the oil and swirl to coat the base and side. Cook the spring onion for 1–2 minutes, or until lightly golden, then remove from the wok. Add the coconut cream to the wok and bring to the boil over high heat, then simmer for 10 minutes, or until the oil starts to separate from the cream (this is called cracking).

4 Stir in the processed paste and then simmer over medium heat for 1–2 minutes, until fragrant. Add the stock, lemon grass, coconut milk, pumpkin and cooked spring onion, cover and simmer for 8–10 minutes, until the pumpkin is tender. Add the prawns and cook, uncovered, for a further 2–3 minutes, or until cooked through. Stir in the fish sauce and basil and serve.

250 g (9 oz) small raw prawns (shrimp)
½ teaspoon shrimp paste
2 long red chillies, chopped
¼ teaspoon white peppercorns
2 tablespoons chilli paste
2 garlic cloves
3 teaspoons oil
5 spring onions (scallions), sliced
125 ml (4 fl oz/½ cup) coconut cream
500 ml (17 fl oz/2 cups) chicken stock
2 lemon grass stems, white part only, bruised
875 ml (30 fl oz/3½ cups) coconut milk
750 g (1 lb 10 oz) pumpkin (winter squash), cut into 2 cm (¾ inch) cubes
1 tablespoon fish sauce
4 tablespoons Thai basil leaves

Hoisin beef stew

»PREPARATION 15 MINUTES »COOKING TIME 1 HOUR 45 MINUTES »SERVES 6

1 Heat a wok until very hot, add the peanut oil and swirl to coat the base and side. Stir-fry the beef in batches for 1–2 minutes, or until browned all over. Remove from the wok and set aside.

2 Add the ginger and garlic to the wok and stir-fry for a few seconds. Add the stock, rice wine, hoisin sauce, cassia bark, tangerine peel, star anise, sichuan peppercorns, sugar, daikon and 875 ml (30 fl oz/ 3½ cups) water then return all of the beef to the wok. Bring to the boil, skimming any scum that forms on the surface, then reduce the heat until simmering and cook, stirring occasionally for 1½ hours, or until the beef is tender and the sauce has thickened slightly. Add the spring onion and the bamboo shoots 5 minutes before the end of the cooking time. Stir in a few drops of sesame oil and garnish with extra spring onion, if desired. Serve with steamed rice.

Note You can remove the star anise, cassia bark and tangerine peel before serving or leave them in the serving dish for presentation.

1½ tablespoons peanut oil

1 kg (2 lb 2 oz) beef chuck steak, cut into 3 cm (1¼ inch) cubes

1 tablespoon finely chopped fresh ginger

1 tablespoon finely chopped garlic

1 litre (35 fl oz/4 cups) beef stock

80 ml (2½ fl oz/⅓ cup) Chinese rice wine

80 ml (2½ fl oz/⅓ cup) hoisin sauce

5 cm (2 inch) piece cassia bark

1 piece dried tangerine peel

2 star anise

1 teaspoon sichuan peppercorns, lightly crushed

2 teaspoons brown sugar

300 g (10½ oz) daikon, cut into 3 cm (1¼ inch) chunks

3 spring onions (scallions), cut into 3 cm (1¼ inch) lengths, plus extra, to garnish

50 g (1¾ oz) tinned bamboo shoots, sliced

a few drops sesame oil (optional)

steamed rice, to serve

North Vietnamese braised pork leg

»PREPARATION 30 MINUTES + MARINATING   »COOKING TIME 1 HOUR 45 MINUTES   »SERVES 4–6

1 Heat a wok until very hot, add 2 teaspoons of the oil and swirl to coat the base and side. Put the pork leg in the wok, skin side down, and cook for 2 minutes, or until well browned. Turn and cook the other side for a further 2 minutes, or until browned. Remove and set aside to cool. Cut the pork leg into 3 cm (1¼ inch) cubes.

2 Preheat the grill (broiler) to high, wrap the shrimp paste in foil, and cook under the grill for 5 minutes. Cool, remove the foil, then put the paste in a large bowl with the garlic, red shallots, galangal, turmeric, sugar and fish sauce and mix well. Add the pork to the bowl and coat it in the marinade. Cover the pork and refrigerate for 1–2 hours.

3 Heat the wok until hot, add the remaining oil and swirl to coat. Add the pork and stir-fry in batches for 1–2 minutes, until browned. Pour in the stock mixture and vinegar, and simmer, covered, over low heat for 1½ hours, or until very tender. Skim the surface often to remove any fat and scum that floats to the surface.

4 Combine the cornflour with 1 teaspoon water to make a paste. Remove the pork from the liquid with a slotted spoon and set aside. Bring the remaining stock to a simmer and skim the surface. Mix in the cornflour paste. Simmer for 2 minutes, or until thickened, then return the pork to the wok and add the spring onion. Season and serve.

1½ tablespoons vegetable oil
1 kg (2 lb 4 oz) boned pork leg in one piece, skin and fat intact
1 teaspoon shrimp paste
5 garlic cloves, crushed
3 red Asian shallots, finely chopped
3 teaspoons ground galangal
1 teaspoon ground turmeric
2 teaspoons sugar
2 tablespoons fish sauce
500 ml (17 fl oz/2 cups) beef stock diluted with 200 ml (7 fl oz) water
2 tablespoons Chinese black vinegar
1 teaspoon cornflour (cornstarch)
3 spring onions (scallions), thinly sliced

Clay pot chicken
and vegetables

»PREPARATION 20 MINUTES + MARINATING »COOKING TIME 35 MINUTES »SERVES 4

1 Wash the chicken under cold water and pat dry with paper towel. Cut the chicken into small pieces. Put it in a dish with the soy sauce and sherry, cover and marinate for 30 minutes in the refrigerator.

2 Cover the dried mushrooms with hot water and soak for 20 minutes. Drain and squeeze to remove any excess liquid. Remove the stems and chop the caps into shreds.

3 Drain the chicken, reserving the marinade. Heat half the oil in a wok, swirling gently to coat the base and side. Add half the chicken pieces and stir-fry briefly until seared on all sides. Transfer to a flameproof clay pot or casserole dish. Stir-fry the remaining chicken and add it to the clay pot.

4 Heat the remaining peanut oil in the wok. Add the leek and ginger and stir-fry for 1 minute. Add the mushrooms, remaining marinade, stock and sesame oil and cook for 2 minutes. Transfer to the clay pot with the sweet potato and cook, covered, on the top of the stove over very low heat for about 20 minutes.

5 Dissolve the cornflour in a little water and add it to the pot. Cook, stirring over high heat, until the mixture boils and thickens. Serve the chicken and vegetables at once with steamed rice.

Note Like all stews, this is best cooked 1–2 days ahead and stored, covered, in the refrigerator to allow the flavours to mature. It can also be frozen, but omit the sweet potato. Steam or boil the potato separately when the dish is reheating and stir it through.

500 g (1 lb 2 oz) boneless, skinless chicken thighs
1 tablespoon soy sauce
1 tablespoon dry sherry
6 dried Chinese mushrooms
2 tablespoons peanut oil
2 small leeks, white part only, sliced
5 cm (2 inch) piece fresh ginger, grated
125 ml (4 fl oz/½ cup) chicken stock
1 teaspoon sesame oil
250 g (9 oz) orange sweet potato, sliced
3 teaspoons cornflour (cornstarch)
steamed rice, to serve

Chinese combination short soup

1 Put all the stock ingredients in a stockpot and cover with 4 litres (140 fl oz/16 cups) water. Bring to the boil over high heat and skim off any scum that forms on the surface. Reduce the heat and simmer for 2 hours.

2 Cool slightly, then remove the chicken and strain the stock into a bowl. Cover and refrigerate the chicken meat and stock separately until chilled. Skim off the fat from the top of the stock.

3 Meanwhile, remove one breast from the chicken, then discard the skin and thinly slice the flesh. Peel the prawns and gently pull out the dark vein from each prawn back, starting from the head end.

4 Pour 2 litres (70 fl oz/8 cups) of the stock into a large wok and bring to the boil. Add the won tons and cook for 2–3 minutes, until they have risen to the surface and are cooked through. Remove with a slotted spoon and divide among serving bowls. Reduce the stock to a simmer, add the prawns, pork, mushrooms and bamboo shoots and cook for 30 seconds, or until the prawns are just curled. Add the bok choy, spring onion, chicken and the combined soy sauce, oyster sauce and sesame oil and cook for 2 minutes, or until the prawns are completely cooked. Ladle the soup over the won tons and serve.

Stock

1.5 kg (3 lb 5 oz) whole chicken
60 ml (2 fl oz/¼ cup) Chinese rice wine
½ star anise
8 spring onions (scallions), chopped
2 leafy celery tops
½ teaspoon white peppercorns
4 garlic cloves, bruised
2 x 10 cm (¾ x 4 inch) piece fresh
  ginger, thinly sliced

12 raw prawns (shrimp)
24 won tons
200 g (7 oz) Chinese barbecued pork,
  thinly sliced
60 g (2¼ oz) Chinese straw
  mushrooms
70 g (2½ oz) sliced bamboo shoots
500 g (1 lb 2 oz) baby bok choy
  (pak choy), thinly sliced
2 spring onions (scallions), cut into
  3 cm (1¼ inch) lengths
2½ tablespoons light soy sauce
1 tablespoon oyster sauce
½ teaspoon sesame oil

Chicken soup with vermicelli

» PREPARATION 15 MINUTES
» COOKING TIME 45 MINUTES » SERVES 4

1 Combine 1 kg (2 lb 4 oz) chicken pieces and 1.5 litres (52 fl oz/6 cups) water in a saucepan. Bring to the boil and skim off any scum. Add 6 chopped spring onions (scallions), a very finely sliced 2 cm (¾ inch) piece of fresh ginger, 2 bay leaves and 2 tablespoons soy sauce. Season with ¼ teaspoon each of salt and pepper, and simmer for 30 minutes.

2 Put 100 g (3½ oz) of dried rice vermicelli in a heatproof bowl, cover with boiling water and soak for 10 minutes, or until soft. Drain.

3 Arrange the vermicelli, 50 g (1¾ oz) chopped English spinach, 2 thinly sliced celery stalks and 200 g (7 oz) of trimmed bean sprouts on a platter. To serve, each diner puts a serving of vermicelli and a selection of vegetables in a large bowl. Pour the chicken soup, including a couple of pieces of chicken, into each bowl. Sprinkle with crisp fried onion and season with chilli sauce.

Vietnamese beef pho

» PREPARATION 15 MINUTES
» COOKING TIME 35 MINUTES » SERVES 4

1 Stud half an onion with 2 cloves. Slice a 4 cm (1½ inch) piece of ginger. Put 2 litres (70 fl oz/8 cups) beef stock, the onion, ginger, 1 star anise, 2 bruised lemon grass stems, 2 crushed garlic cloves, 2 halved pigs' trotters and ¼ teaspoon ground white pepper in a wok. Bring to the boil. Reduce the heat and simmer, covered, for 30 minutes. Strain the broth, then return to the wok and stir in 1 tablespoon fish sauce.

2 Thinly slice 300 g (10½ oz) partially frozen beef fillet. Put 200 g (7 oz) fresh thin rice noodles in a heatproof bowl, cover with boiling water and gently separate. Drain and divide the noodles among four bowls then top with the beef, 90 g (3¼ oz/1 cup) bean sprouts, 2 sliced spring onions (scallions), 25 g (1 oz) chopped coriander (cilantro) leaves, 4 tablespoons chopped Vietnamese mint and 1 thinly sliced red chilli. Ladle over the broth. Serve with extra fish sauce and lime quarters.

Scallops with soba noodles

» PREPARATION 10 MINUTES
» COOKING TIME 15 MINUTES » SERVES 4

1 Add 250 g (9 oz) dried soba noodles to a large pan of boiling water and stir to separate. Return to the boil, adding 250 ml (9 fl oz/ 1 cup) cold water. Repeat this step three times, as it comes to the boil. Drain and rinse under cold water.

2 Put 875 ml (30 fl oz/3½ cups) water, 60 ml (2 fl oz/¼ cup) mirin, 60 ml (2 fl oz/¼ cup) light soy sauce, 2 teaspoons rice vinegar and 1 teaspoon dashi granules in a non-stick wok. Bring to the boil, then simmer for 3–4 minutes. Add 2 sliced spring onions (scallions) and 1 teaspoon finely chopped fresh ginger and keep at a gentle simmer.

3 Sear 24 large scallops in a very hot chargrill pan for 30 seconds on each side. Divide the noodles and 5 chopped fresh black fungus (or dried, soaked in warm water for 20 minutes) among four bowls. Add the broth and top with the scallops. Garnish with shredded nori.

Fish ball and noodle soup

»PREPARATION 15 MINUTES »COOKING TIME 15 MINUTES »SERVES 4–6

1 Put the fish in a food processor and process until smooth. Combine the rice flour and 80 ml (2½ fl oz/ ⅓ cup) water until smooth, add to the fish and process for 5 seconds. Using 2 teaspoons of mixture at a time, shape the fish mixture into balls with wet hands.

2 Cook the somen noodles in a large saucepan of boiling water for 2 minutes, or until tender. Drain and set aside.

3 Pour 2 litres (70 fl oz/8 cups) of water into a non-stick wok. Bring to the boil, then reduce the heat to low, add the dashi granules and stir until dissolved. Increase the heat to high

and bring to the boil, then add the soy sauce, mirin and salt to taste. Add the fish balls, reduce the heat and simmer for 3 minutes, or until they rise to the surface and are cooked through. Add the Chinese cabbage, increase the heat to high and return to the boil. Stir in the noodles and cook for 1 minute, or until warmed through.

4 To serve, divide the noodles and fish balls among serving bowls then ladle the hot liquid over the top. Garnish with the spring onion and cucumber strips.

500 g (1 lb 2 oz) skinless, boneless firm white fish fillets, such as ling or perch
2 tablespoons rice flour
200 g (7 oz) dried somen noodles
2½ teaspoons dashi granules
2 tablespoons light soy sauce
1 tablespoon mirin
200 g (7 oz) Chinese cabbage (wong bok), shredded
2 spring onions (scallions), thinly sliced, to garnish
½ Lebanese (short) cucumber, peeled, seeded and cut into 5 cm (2 inch) strips

Thai sweet and sour chicken soup

»PREPARATION 20 MINUTES »COOKING TIME 20 MINUTES »SERVES 4–6

1 Soak the chillies in the boiling water for 20 minutes, then drain and chop. Put the chilli, shallot, garlic, galangal, turmeric, lemon grass, lime zest and shrimp paste in a food processor or blender and blend to a smooth paste, adding a little water if necessary.

2 Put the chicken stock and 250 ml (9 fl oz/1 cup) water in a non-stick wok, add the whole makrut leaves and bring to the boil over high heat. Stir in the blended chilli paste and simmer for 5 minutes.

3 Add the tamarind, fish sauce, palm sugar, chicken, asparagus and corn and stir to prevent the chicken clumping. Simmer for 10 minutes, or until the chicken is cooked and the vegetables are tender. Stir in the pineapple cubes before serving in individual bowls.

Note Use a non-stick or stainless steel wok for this recipe because the tamarind purée reacts with a regular wok and will taint the whole dish.

6 large dried red chillies
250 ml (9 fl oz/1 cup) boiling water
4 red Asian shallots, chopped
4 garlic cloves, chopped
2 tablespoons chopped fresh galangal
2 teaspoons chopped fresh turmeric
2 lemon grass stems, white part only, finely chopped
½ teaspoon grated lime zest
1 teaspoon shrimp paste
1 litre (35 fl oz/4 cups) chicken stock
6 makrut (kaffir lime) leaves
2 tablespoons tamarind purée
2 tablespoons fish sauce
30 g (1 oz/¼ cup) grated palm sugar (jaggery) or soft brown sugar
450 g (1 lb) boneless, skinless chicken breast, thinly sliced
200 g (7 oz) asparagus, woody ends trimmed and cut into thirds
100 g (3½ oz) baby corn, cut in half lengthways
200 g (7 oz) fresh pineapple, cut into 2 cm (¾ inch) cubes

Pork and corn ramen noodle soup

»PREPARATION 15 MINUTES »COOKING TIME 30 MINUTES »SERVES 4

1 Cut the pork into thin slices. Cut the kernels from the corn cobs.

2 Cook the ramen noodles in a large saucepan of boiling water for 4 minutes, or until tender. Drain, rinse in cold water then drain again. Set aside.

3 Heat a wok over high heat, add the oil and swirl to coat the base and side. Stir-fry the ginger for 1–2 minutes, then add the chicken stock, mirin and 500 ml (17 fl oz/ 2 cups) water. Bring to the boil, reduce the heat and simmer for 6–8 minutes. Add the pork to the broth and cook for 5 minutes. Add the corn kernels and spring onion and cook for a further 4–5 minutes, or until the kernels are tender.

4 Separate the noodles by running them under hot water, then divide among four deep bowls, shaping them into mounds. Ladle over the liquid and top with the pork and corn. Put 1 teaspoon butter on top of each mound and garnish with the spring onion. Serve immediately.

200 g (7 oz) Chinese barbecued pork fillet, in one piece
2 small fresh corn cobs
200 g (7 oz) dried ramen noodles
2 teaspoons peanut oil
1 teaspoon grated fresh ginger
1.5 litres (52 fl oz/6 cups) chicken stock
2 tablespoons mirin
2 spring onions (scallions), sliced
20 g (¾ oz) unsalted butter
1 spring onion (scallion), sliced, extra, to serve

Sichuan beef noodle soup

»PREPARATION 10 MINUTES »COOKING TIME 3 HOURS »SERVES 4

1 Pour the beef stock and 2 litres (70 fl oz/8 cups) of water into a stockpot. Simmer over low heat; keep warm until needed

2 Heat a wok over high heat, add the oil and swirl to coat the base and side. Add the steak and sear it for 2–3 minutes on each side. Add the cinnamon stick, star anise, peppercorns, ginger, soy sauce, rice wine, bean sauce and the mandarin peel. Pour in the broth, then cover and bring to simmering point over medium heat. Reduce the heat and simmer, covered, for 2–2½ hours, until the steak is tender (you should be able to shred it; if not, return to the simmer until tender).

3 Remove the steak and discard the mandarin peel. Meanwhile, cook the noodles in a large pan of boiling water for 1 minute to separate them. Drain. Just before serving, add the noodles to the broth and let them stand for 1–2 minutes, or until heated through. Shred the steak into bite-sized pieces and divide among four large serving bowls. Ladle on the broth and noodles, sprinkle with spring onion and serve.

Note Dried citrus peel is one of the most important Chinese flavourings and the dried peel of mandarins, tangerines and oranges is sold at many Asian food stores.

1.5 litres (52 fl oz/6 cups) beef stock
1 tablespoon peanut oil
400 g (14 oz) beef chuck steak
½ cinnamon stick
2 star anise
1½ teaspoons sichuan peppercorns, crushed
1 tablespoon finely sliced fresh ginger
2 tablespoons dark soy sauce
1 tablespoon Chinese rice wine
1 tablespoon brown bean sauce
3 x 5 cm (1¼ x 2 inch) piece dried mandarin peel (see Note)
125 g (4½ oz) fresh thin egg noodles
3 spring onions (scallions), thinly sliced

Shanghai chicken and noodle soup

»PREPARATION 10 MINUTES »COOKING TIME 35 MINUTES »SERVES 4–6

1 Pour the stock into a non-stick wok and bring to the boil. Reduce to medium–low heat and add the star anise and ginger slices. Poach the chicken for 15–20 minutes, or until cooked through. Remove the chicken with a slotted spoon and set aside to cool. Leave the stock in the wok.

2 Meanwhile, bring 2 litres (70 fl oz/8 cups) water to the boil in a large saucepan and cook the noodles for 3 minutes. Drain and refresh under cold water.

3 Cut the chicken across the breast into 5 mm (¼ inch) slices. Return the stock to the boil and add the asparagus, ginger, soy sauce, rice wine, sugar and ½ teaspoon salt. Reduce the heat, add the noodles and simmer for 2 minutes. Return the chicken to the wok and cook for 1 minute, until heated through.

4 Remove the noodles from the liquid with tongs and evenly divide among serving bowls. Divide the chicken, asparagus, spring onion and watercress (if using) among the bowls, then ladle the broth on top. Drizzle with sesame oil and serve with extra soy sauce, if desired.

2 litres (70 fl oz/8 cups) ready-made chicken stock diluted with 500 ml (17 fl oz/2 cups) water

1 star anise

4 thin slices fresh ginger

600 g (1 lb 5 oz) boneless, skinless chicken breasts

375 g (13 oz) Shanghai noodles

200 g (7 oz) fresh asparagus, woody ends trimmed, cut into 3 cm (1 ¼ inch) pieces

1 tablespoon finely sliced fresh ginger

1 ½ tablespoons light soy sauce

1 tablespoon Chinese rice wine

½ teaspoon sugar

4 spring onions (scallions), thinly sliced on the diagonal

50 g (1 ¾ oz) watercress tips (optional)

¼ teaspoon sesame oil, to drizzle

soy sauce, extra, to serve (optional)

84 Kheer rice pudding

85 Eight-treasure rice

88 Egg tarts

92 Thai sticky rice with mangoes

93 Green tea ice cream

Desserts

Kheer rice pudding

» PREPARATION 15 MINUTES
» COOKING TIME 1 HOUR 50 MINUTES » SERVES 4

1 Soak 65 g (2½ oz/⅓ cup) basmati rice in water for 30 minutes; drain.

2 Pour 1.5 litres (52 fl oz/6 cups) milk into a saucepan, add 6 lightly crushed cardamom pods and bring to the boil. Add the rice, reduce the heat and simmer, stirring often, for 1 hour, or until the rice is cooked.

3 Add 115 g (4 oz/½ cup) caster (superfine) sugar to the rice, along with 40 g (1½ oz/¼ cup) chopped raisins and 30 g (1 oz/¼ cup) of slivered almonds. Bring to a low boil and cook for 50 minutes, until it is the consistency of porridge. Stir often to prevent sticking. Discard the cardamom pods.

4 Mix a pinch of saffron threads with a little water and add to the mixture — just enough to give a pale yellow colour to the pudding. Stir in 1 tablespoon rosewater, if desired, when cooled. Serve warm or cold, with a sprinkling of ground cinnamon on top, if desired.

Sweet won tons

» PREPARATION 15 MINUTES
» COOKING TIME 20 MINUTES » MAKES 30

1 Combine 125 g (4½ oz) pitted, chopped dates, 2 finely chopped bananas, 45 g (1¾ oz/½ cup) lightly crushed flaked almonds and ½ teaspoon ground cinnamon.

2 Spoon 2 teaspoons of the fruit mixture on the centre of 30 won ton wrappers. Lightly brush the edges with water and top with another 30 won ton wrappers at an angle so that the wrappers make a star shape. Put the won tons in a single layer on a tray lined with baking paper.

3 Fill a deep-fryer or large heavy-based saucepan one-third full of oil and heat to 180°C (350°F/Gas 4), or until a cube of bread dropped into the oil browns in 15 seconds. Deep-dry won tons, in batches, for 2 minutes, or until crisp and golden. Drain on paper towel. Lightly dust won tons with icing (confectioners') sugar before serving.

Chinese fortune cookies

» PREPARATION 40 MINUTES
» COOKING TIME 50 MINUTES » MAKES 30

1 Preheat the oven to 180°C (350°F/Gas 4) and line a baking tray with baking paper. Draw three 8 cm (3¼ inch) circles on the paper.

2 Whisk 3 egg whites until just frothy. Sift 60 g (2¼ oz/½ cup) icing (confectioners') sugar onto the egg whites and add 45 g (1½ oz) melted unsalted butter. Stir until smooth. Add 60 g (2¼ oz/½ cup) of plain (all-purpose) flour and mix until smooth. Stand for 15 minutes.

3 Spread 1½ level teaspoons of the mixture over each circle. Bake for 5 minutes, or until slightly brown around the edges. Working quickly, remove the cookies from the tray by sliding a flat-bladed knife under each. Put a written fortune message on each cookie. Fold the cookie in half to form a semi-circle, then fold again over a blunt-edged object like the rim of a glass. Cool on a wire rack. Repeat with the remaining cookie mixture.

Eight-treasure rice

1 Soak the lotus seeds and jujubes in separate bowls of cold water for 30 minutes, then drain. Remove the seeds from the jujubes. Blanch the fresh gingko nuts in boiling water for 5 minutes, then refresh in cold water and dry thoroughly.

2 Put the glutinous rice and 300 ml (10½ fl oz) water in a heavy-based saucepan and bring to the boil. Reduce the heat to low and simmer for 10–15 minutes. Stir in the sugar and oil.

3 Dissolve the slab sugar in 210 ml (7½ fl oz) of water and bring to the boil. Add the lotus seeds, jujubes and gingko nuts and simmer for 1 hour, or until the lotus seeds are soft. Drain, reserving the liquid.

4 Grease a 1 litre (35 fl oz/4 cup) heatproof bowl and decorate the base with the lotus seeds, jujubes, gingko nuts, cherries, longans and almonds. Smooth two-thirds of the rice over this to form a shell. Fill with the bean paste. Cover with the remaining rice; smooth the surface.

5 Cover the rice with greased foil and put the bowl in a steamer. Cover and steam over simmering water in a wok for 1–1½ hours, replenishing with boiling water as needed. Turn the pudding out onto a plate and pour the reserved sugar liquid over the top. Serve hot.

Notes Lotus seeds are the seeds from the lotus and are available from Asian grocery stores.

Jujubes (Chinese dates) are a dried fruit with a red, wrinkled skin.

Gingko nuts are the nuts of the maidenhair tree. The hard shells are cracked open and the inner nuts soaked to loosen their skins. Shelled nuts can be bought in tins and are easier to use than unshelled ones.

Longans are from the same family as lychees. They are available fresh, tinned or dried.

12 whole blanched lotus seeds (see Notes)
12 jujubes (dried Chinese dates) (see Notes)
20 fresh or tinned gingko nuts, shelled (see Notes)
225 g (8 oz) glutinous rice
2 tablespoons sugar
2 teaspoons oil
30 g (1 oz) slab sugar
8 glacé (candied) cherries
6 dried longans, pitted (see Notes)
4 almonds or walnuts
225 g (8 oz) red bean paste

Spicy coconut custard

»PREPARATION 20 MINUTES »COOKING TIME 1 HOUR »SERVES 8

1 Preheat the oven to 160°C (315°F/ Gas 2–3). Combine the cinnamon, nutmeg, cloves, cream and 250 ml (9 fl oz/1 cup) water in a saucepan. Heat until simmering, then reduce the heat to very low and leave for 5 minutes for the spices to infuse the liquid. Add the palm sugar and coconut milk and stir over low heat until the sugar has dissolved.

2 Whisk the eggs and egg yolks in a bowl until combined. Stir in the spiced cream mixture, then strain, discarding the whole spices. Pour into eight 125 ml (4 fl oz/¼ cup)

ramekins or dariole moulds. Place in a baking dish and pour in enough hot water to come halfway up the sides of the ramekins. Bake the custards for 40–45 minutes, until set. The custards should wobble slightly when the dish is shaken lightly. Remove the custards from the baking dish. Serve hot or chilled with whipped cream and toasted coconut sprinkled over the top.

2 cinnamon sticks
1 teaspoon freshly grated nutmeg
2 teaspoons cloves
310 ml (10¾ fl oz/1¼ cups) pouring (whipping) cream
90 g (3¼ oz) chopped palm sugar (jaggery), or soft brown sugar
270 ml (9½ fl oz) coconut milk
3 eggs, lightly beaten
2 egg yolks, lightly beaten
whipped cream, to serve
toasted shredded coconut, to serve

custards should wobble slightly...

Lemon and lime sorbet

» PREPARATION 25 MINUTES + FREEZING » COOKING TIME 10 MINUTES » SERVES 4

1 Put 500 ml (17 fl oz/2 cups) of water and 220 g (7¾ oz/1 cup) sugar in a saucepan and stir over low heat until the sugar has dissolved. Bring to the boil, reduce the heat to low and simmer for 5 minutes. Cool. Add 185 ml (6 fl oz/¾ cup) lemon juice and 185 ml (6 fl oz/¾ cup) lime juice to the syrup.

2 Transfer the syrup to an ice cream machine. Freeze according to the manufacturer's instructions. Add 2 lightly beaten egg whites when the sorbet is almost churned and the machine is still running.

3 Alternatively, transfer the syrup to a shallow metal tray, cover with a piece of baking paper and freeze for 2 hours. Transfer the icy mixture to a food processor or bowl and process or beat with electric beaters to a slush, then return to the freezer. Repeat the beating and freezing twice more. Transfer to a bowl or food processor. With electric beaters or with the food processor's motor running, add 2 lightly beaten egg whites and blend. Return the sorbet to the freezer container, cover with a piece of baking paper and freeze until firm.

Egg tarts

1 To make the outer dough, sift the flour and icing sugar into a bowl. Make a well in the centre. Combine the oil with 80 ml (2½ oz/⅓ cup) of water and pour the mixture into the dry ingredients. Mix with a flat-bladed knife, using a cutting action, to form a rough dough. (If the flour is very dry, add a little extra water.) Turn the dough out onto a lightly floured surface and gather together in a smooth ball. Cover and set aside for 15 minutes.

2 To make the inner dough, sift the flour into a bowl. Using your fingertips, rub the lard into the flour until the mixture resembles breadcrumbs. Press the dough together into a ball, cover and set aside for 15 minutes.

3 On a lightly floured surface, roll the outer dough into a rectangle about 10 x 20 cm (4 x 8 inches). Roll the inner dough into a smaller rectangle, one-third the size of the outer dough. Place the inner dough in the centre of the outer dough. Fold the outer dough over the inner dough so the short edges overlap and the inner dough is enclosed. Pinch the edges together to seal. Roll the dough away from you in one direction into a long rectangle, until it is about half as thick as it was previously. Fold the pastry into three layers by taking the left-hand edge over first, and then folding the right-hand edge over the top. Wrap the dough in plastic wrap and chill for 30 minutes. Preheat the oven to 210°C (415°F/Gas 6–7). Brush two 12-hole muffin tins with melted butter or oil.

4 To make the custard, place 80 ml (2½ oz/⅓ cup) water and the sugar in a saucepan. Stir, without boiling, until the sugar dissolves. Bring to a boil and simmer, without stirring, for 1 minute. Cool the mixture for 5 minutes. Put the eggs in a bowl and beat lightly with a fork. Whisk the sugar syrup into the eggs until just combined. Strain.

5 Put the pastry on a lightly floured surface. With one open end towards you, roll the pastry into a rectangle about 3 mm (⅛ inch) thick. Cut out rounds from the pastry using a 7 cm (2¾ inch) fluted cutter. Carefully place the pastry rounds into the patty pans and fill two-thirds full with the egg custard mixture. Bake for 15 minutes, or until just set. Be careful not to overcook the custard. Leave the tarts to cool for 3 minutes before removing them from the tin. Cool the tarts on a wire rack, and serve warm or cold.

Outer dough
165 g (5¾ oz/1⅓ cups) plain (all-purpose) flour
2 tablespoons icing (confectioners') sugar
2 tablespoons oil

Inner dough
125 g (4½ oz/1 cup) plain (all-purpose) flour
100 g (3½ oz) lard, chopped

Custard
55 g (2 oz/¼ cup) caster (superfine) sugar
2 eggs

Kulfi

» PREPARATION 20 MINUTES + FREEZING » COOKING TIME 50 MINUTES » SERVES 6

1 Put the milk and cardamom pods in a large heavy-based saucepan. Bring to the boil, then reduce the heat and simmer, stirring often, until the milk has reduced by about one-third — this will take some time. Keep stirring or it will stick.

2 Add the caster sugar and cook for 2–3 minutes. Strain and discard the cardamom pods. Add the nuts. Pour the kulfi into a shallow metal or plastic container, cover the surface with a sheet of baking paper and freeze for 1 hour. Remove from the freezer and beat to break up any ice crystals, freeze again and repeat twice more.

3 Lightly brush six 250 ml (9 fl oz/ 1 cup) pudding basins (moulds) with the oil and divide the kulfi among them, then freeze overnight. To serve, unmould each kulfi and cut a cross 5 mm (¼ inch) deep in the top. Serve with extra pistachio nuts sprinkled over the top.

1.5 litres (52 fl oz/6 cups) milk
8 cardamom pods
4 tablespoons caster (superfine) sugar
20 g (¾ oz) blanched almonds, finely chopped
20 g (¾ oz) pistachio nuts, chopped, plus extra, to garnish
vegetable oil, for greasing

New Year sweet dumplings

» PREPARATION 40 MINUTES » COOKING TIME 15 MINUTES » MAKES 24

1 Combine the sesame paste with the caster sugar in a small bowl.

2 Sift the rice flour into a bowl and stir in the boiling water. Knead carefully (the dough will be hot) to form a soft, slightly sticky dough. Dust your hands with extra rice flour, roll the dough into a cylinder and then divide it into cherry-size pieces. Cover the dough with a tea towel (dish towel) and, using one piece at a time, form each piece of dough into a flat round, then gather it into a cup shape. The dough should be fairly thin.

3 Fill each cup shape with about 1 teaspoon of the sesame paste and fold the top over, smoothing the

dough so that you have a smooth round ball with no visible joins.

4 Bring 1 litre (35 fl oz/4 cups) of water to the boil, add the rock sugar and stir until dissolved. Return to the boil, then add the dumplings in batches and simmer for 5 minutes, or until they rise to the surface. Serve the dumplings warm with a little of the syrup.

Note Yellow rock sugar comes as uneven lumps of sugar, which may need to be further crushed before use if very big. It is a pure sugar that produces a clear syrup and makes sauces shiny and clear. You can use sugar cubes instead.

60 g (2¼ oz) black sesame paste, red bean paste or smooth peanut butter
80 g (2¾ oz/⅓ cup) caster (superfine) sugar
250 g (9 oz) glutinous rice flour
220 ml (7¾ fl oz) boiling water
30 g (1 oz) yellow rock sugar (see Note)

Thai sticky rice with mangoes

»PREPARATION 10 MINUTES + SOAKING »COOKING TIME 1 HOUR 5 MINUTES »SERVES 4

1 Put the rice in a sieve and wash under cold running water until the water runs clear. Put the rice in a glass or ceramic bowl, cover with water and soak overnight, or for at least 12 hours. Drain the rice.

2 Line a metal or bamboo steamer with a piece of muslin (cheesecloth). Put the drained rice on top of the muslin and cover the steamer with a tight-fitting lid. Put the steamer over a saucepan or wok of boiling water and steam over medium–low heat for 50 minutes, or until the rice is cooked. Replenish the pot with boiling water as necessary. Transfer the rice to a large bowl and fluff it up with a fork.

3 Toast the sesame seeds in a dry frying pan over medium heat for 3–4 minutes, shaking the pan gently until the seeds are golden brown. Remove from the pan immediately to prevent them burning.

4 Put the coconut milk in a small saucepan, then add the palm sugar and ¼ teaspoon of salt. Slowly bring the mixture to the boil, stirring constantly until the palm sugar has dissolved. Reduce the heat and then simmer for 5 minutes, or until the mixture is slightly thickened. Stir the mixture often during cooking, to prevent it sticking to the bottom of the pan.

5 Slowly pour the coconut milk over the top of the rice. Use a fork to lift and fluff up the rice. Do not stir the liquid through, otherwise the rice will become too gluggy. Let the rice mixture rest for 20 minutes before carefully spooning it into the centre of four warmed serving bowls. Arrange the mango slices on the rice mounds. Spoon a little coconut cream over the sticky rice, sprinkle over the sesame seeds and garnish with the mint.

400 g (14 oz/2 cups) long-grain white rice
1 tablespoon white sesame seeds
250 ml (9 fl oz/1 cup) coconut milk
70 g (2½ oz/½ cup) grated palm sugar (jaggery)
2–3 mangoes, peeled, seeded and sliced
60 ml (2 fl oz/¼ cup) coconut cream
mint sprigs, to garnish

Green tea ice cream

»PREPARATION 15 MINUTES + FREEZING »COOKING TIME 30 MINUTES »SERVES 4

1 Combine the green tea leaves with the milk in a saucepan and slowly bring to simmering point. This step should not be rushed — the longer the milk takes to come to a simmer, the better the infusion of flavour. Set aside for 5 minutes before straining.

2 Whisk the egg yolks and sugar in a heatproof bowl until thick and pale, then add the infused milk. Place the bowl over a saucepan of simmering water, making sure that the base of the bowl does not touch the water. Stir the custard until it is thick enough to coat the back of spoon, then remove from the heat and allow to cool slightly before stirring through the cream. Transfer to an ice cream machine and freeze according to the manufacturer's instructions. Alternatively, transfer the mixture to a shallow metal tray and freeze, whisking every couple of hours until frozen and creamy. Freeze overnight.

Note If you prefer your green tea ice cream pale green, add a few drops of green food colouring.

4 tablespoons Japanese green
    tea leaves
500 ml (17 fl oz/2 cups) milk
6 egg yolks
115 g (4 oz/½ cup) caster (superfine)
    sugar
500 ml (17 fl oz/2 cups) pouring
    (whipping) cream

Index

Published in 2011 by Murdoch Books Pty Limited.

Murdoch Books Australia
Pier 8/9, 23 Hickson Road, Millers Point NSW 2000
Phone: +61 (0)2 8220 2000 Fax: +61 (0)2 8220 2558
www.murdochbooks.com.au

Murdoch Books UK Limited
Erico House, 6th Floor North, 93–99 Upper Richmond Road
Putney, London SW15 2TG
Phone: + 44 (0) 20 8785 5995 Fax: + 44 (0) 20 8785 5985
www.murdochbooks.co.uk

Publisher Lynn Lewis
Design Concept Adam Walker
Designer Lena Lowe
Editor Justine Harding
Project Manager Liz Malcolm
Production Alexandra Gonzalez

National Library of Australia Cataloguing-in-Publication Data:
Title: Easy Asian: a classic kitchen collection for the busy cook.
ISBN: 978-1-74266-423-1 (pbk.)
Series: MB test kitchen favourites.
Notes: Includes index.
Subjects: Cooking (Asian).
Dewey Number: 641.595

Printed by C & C Offset Printing Co. Ltd, China